From the Source

From the Source
Memories of Mago Gilson

Margarita Moreno Zárate

Translated by

Jon Dell Jaramillo

Yachay Kallay Publishers, LLC

From the Source

From the Source

Margarita Moreno Zárate

Translated by Jon Dell Jaramillo

Prologue by Erin Gallo

© 2025 Yachay Kallay Publishing, LLC

All rights reserved. No part of this publication may be reproduced, stored in a retrieval system, or transmitted in any form or by any means, electronic, mechanical, photocopying, recording or otherwise without the prior permission of the publisher or in accordance with the provisions of the Copyright, Designs and Patents Act 1988 or under the terms of any license permitting limited copying issued by the Copyright Licensing Agency.

Published by:
Yachay Kallay Publishing, LLC
2544 Washington Street
Eugene, Oregon 97405 USA

Typesetting: Jon Dell Jaramillo

Cover Design: Margarita Moreno Zárate (needle point)

A CIP record for this book is available from the Library of Congress Cataloging-in-Publication Data

ISBN-13: 979-8-9920538-2-1

From the Source

Contents

Translator's Foreword 9
Prologue 13
Dedication 15
Acknowledgments 17
Author's Note 19
Chapter 1 – Twists of Fate 21
Chapter 2 – Humble Beginnings 27
Chapter 3 – The Most Delicious Coffee 29
Chapter 4 – Our First Mansion 31
Chapter 5 – Everyone but Me 37
Chapter 6 – The First Stone 39
Chapter 7 – A Window for Mama 43
Chapter 8 – My Father's Surprise 47
Chapter 9 – We Didn't Know We Were Poor 53
Chapter 10 – My Tree and I 57
Chapter 11 – Kaliman and Other Hard Truths 63
Chapter 12 – "La tinguilica" and *My Make-Believe River* 67
Chapter 13 – School Days, Cruel Days 71
Chapter 14 – The Price of the Ride 77
Chapter 15 – Glorious Saturday 81
Chapter 16 – Sweet Bread and Little Sins 85
Chapter 17 – The ignored *quinceañera* 89
Chapter 18 – From the Source 93
Chapter 19 – Chapingo, Glorious Campus 99
Chapter 20 – For my husband 105
Chapter 21 – My fascination 107

Chapter 22 – The Three *Desgracias* (Sort Of) 109

Chapter 23 – Like the Five Fingers of My Hand 117

Chapter 24 – The Changes Life Brings 123

Family Album 129

Translator's Foreword

Translating this memoir has been a singular joy and a profound responsibility. *From the Source* is far more than a collection of personal stories; it is like *panderuza y pecaditos*—sweet as freshly baked bread and emotional as an intimate confession—a living archive of voice, place, memory, and cultural inheritance. As I carried these stories from Spanish into English, I became a fellow traveler alongside the narrator—a daughter, sister, mother, immigrant, survivor, and storyteller of great warmth and wit. Her voice, grounded in oral tradition, carries the cadences of a spoken world: full of rhythm, intimacy, digression, and emotional honesty. My task was not only to preserve meaning, but to evoke the feeling of being invited into her kitchen, her memories, and her heart.

Throughout the translation, I made deliberate choices to preserve the tone and humor of the original Spanish, sometimes at the cost of literal phrasing. The narrator's voice blends tenderness, playfulness, nostalgia, indignation, and pride. Much of her humor is rooted in the sound of words—mispronunciations, puns, or invented expressions from childhood. These moments often resist clean translation, but wherever possible I've worked to recreate the spirit, even when the letter could not be carried over. In other cases, the humor emerges from understatement, from cultural irony, or from a well-timed turn of phrase; these, I've rendered with careful attention to rhythm and pause, trusting English to carry their emotional weight.

A notable feature of this translation is the frequent use of the emdash (—), which serves both expressive and pedagogical purposes. The emdash here is more than punctuation—it's part of the narrator's voice. It creates emphasis or surprise at the end of a sentence, marks a dramatic or emotionally weighted aside, and replaces colons when a softer or more lyrical pause is needed. It captures the cadences of spontaneous speech—especially in a memoir rooted in oral tradition—and mirrors the rhythm of a storyteller catching their breath or shifting tones. It also helps signal moments when the voice of the narrator might suddenly turn, exclaim, hesitate, or confide. Readers will find emdashes used to break up long sentences, emphasize contrast, or guide the ear in a way commas or parentheses could not. This is intentional—stylistically and pedagogically—inviting the reader to listen with their eyes.

Certain words, phrases, or names appear in the original Spanish. This decision was not incidental. Language holds more than semantic meaning—it carries a world. Words like *comadre*, *cigüeña*, *mole*, *mija*, or *domingo siete* resist perfect equivalence. Rather than flatten or over-explain them, I've chosen to leave them intact, inviting the English-speaking reader to engage in an act of trust and discovery. You may not understand every word at first, but let the context guide you. Let the story teach you. In this way, the act of reading echoes the experience of migration itself—where language comes alive through need, repetition, love, and risk.

This memoir is rooted in the Mexican oral storytelling tradition, where memory is shared communally, with interruptions, humor, and flourishes. And yet, like the best of literature, it also transcends its particularities. For example, in Chapter 18—*From the Source*—the author expresses the urgency of telling the story before memory fades. Facing such a dilemma, with all its twists and turns of fate, my mind flashed to Cervantes and all the *desgracias* that befell his protagonist Don Quixote and his urgency in living (and telling) the story.

The themes are universal: the ache of growing up, the sting of humiliation, the enduring bonds of family, the quest for dignity, and the radiant resilience of women across generations. The narrator's path—shaped by early motherhood, systemic injustice, migration, and an improbable academic triumph—recalls the spirit of *testimonio* as a literary form, but also bears the intimate realism found in works like Esmeralda Santiago's *When I Was Puerto Rican*, Elena Poniatowska's *Hasta no verte Jesús mío*, or Sandra Cisneros' *The House on Mango Street*.

To English-speaking readers: this memoir will ask something of you. A pause. A little humility. A willingness to feel before you fully understand. It may also give you laughter, tears, and a new friend in its narrator—a woman whose voice is as nourishing as *pan de dulce* and as true as memory itself.

It is my hope that this translation will allow her words to travel across borders, as she once did, carrying not only the weight of the past, but the bright light of her spirit, her storytelling, and her song.

—Jon Dell Jaramillo, PhD
Eugene, Oregon
2025

From the Source

Prologue

The image of the immigrant often only focuses on the moment they cross the border, when in reality that instant weighs less than the millions of moments lived before and after that crossing. Mago Gilson's testimony is a reminder of the crossroads that occur far from the border, hidden in a past both distant and near, in a painful and beautiful youth, and in a past that was and was not, since memory keeps and transforms everything.

Gilson, the eldest of seven siblings, recounts a childhood in Chiapas where small-town rumors, revenge, and machismo reign as vestiges of a past century. At that time, Mexico was immersed in the redistribution of land in the ejidos and the industrialization of cities. Gilson's family experienced these changes when they had to leave their homeland to resettle in the State of Mexico. Although she does not mention it explicitly, Gilson alludes to a fundamental period known as the "Mexican Miracle." The key moments of her memories—such as the construction of her house, the arrival of electricity, schools, television, and radio—are related to this explosion in consumption and the economy experienced by all Mexicans. But, despite this modernization, and like millions of other Mexicans of her time, she lived a humble life, staying on the margins. Amid these harsh realities, Gilson reminds us of the love that existed: "How happy we were! We didn't even know we were poor."

The years are jumbled, just as memory is not a reliable filing system, but between chapters 18 and 20, Gilson reveals her true crossroads. In the first, her mother dies in childbirth while she gives birth to her first daughter, the result of an abusive relationship. Here—an end and a beginning at the same time—Gilson decides to flee to be reborn. From her escape, she becomes a student of life. She starts working and gets new skills to provide for her children. While building her new life as a worker and modern woman, she meets the man who will provoke the second crossroads. She falls in love and, together with her new husband, a US citizen, moves to the United States. For her and for many others, love is the reason for leaving their country.

In her last chapter, Gilson reflects on her extraordinary life. Despite being marginalized from formal education, she managed to obtain a master's degree in education, which led her to be recognized by President Bill Clinton. She freed herself from a harmful relationship and achieved self-sufficiency before meeting her current husband. The most admirable thing about her testimony is the humility with which she narrates her past, reminding us that her lack of opportunities in Mexico was not due to a lack of talent, but to unjust circumstances. By sharing her story, Gilson invites us to reflect on the power of love, resilience, and the ability to transform our lives. Her journey gives us a glimpse into the struggle and hope that define the lives of many immigrants.

—Erin Gallo, PhD
Eugene, Oregon 2024

Dedication

To my beloved children, the most precious treasure of my life; the apples of my eye, Amada and Luzi, and my three dear sons: Óscar, Eddy (Édgar), and Víctor, the youngest. God has given me immense joy by blessing me with you five. Words cannot express the pride I feel for each of you. You are my greatest accomplishment, my reason for being, and the drive behind every step in my life.

With all my love, I dedicate these memories, these anecdotes, and experiences to you. May these pages be a legacy, a treasure that you can share with your own children and grandchildren, because here lies the history of your ancestors, told by the source. It is my deepest wish that these stories go with you and always remind you of where you come from, the love that precedes you, and the strength that is your birthright.

Acknowledgments

First and foremost, I thank God, my creator, guide, and protector. He has given me the words that for years fluttered in my mind, refusing to come out and be printed in these lines. Finally, the ideas flowed and transformed into phrases and sentences that settled here.

My deepest gratitude goes to my family, especially my sisters and my brother; without their love and support, I would not be where I am. With all my love to my dear sisters Lexvia, Clelia, Feliza (up in heaven), Sara, and Lulú, and to my brother Fidel Rey.

I also want to acknowledge my nieces and nephews. Thanks to my niece Rebecca Gutiérrez, who asked me an unexpected question, I felt the urgency to write and set the record straight. The time had come for me to share the reality about how and why things happened. I did not want anyone else to tell it, or have it misinterpreted, or make something up. Here is the long-awaited book. If there are any questions, I'm still here, so ask me!

I feel immense gratitude for my good friend Jon Dell Jaramillo. Without his encouragement and support, this book would still be a dream. When he happened to read one of my pages, still on the computer, he commented that he liked it a lot and that it was material worth publishing. From that comment on, I started to soar high. I worked tirelessly until I finished writing the twenty-four chapters of this book, written with so much love.

I am also grateful to Maria Guadalupe Gutiérrez Cortez for her unconditional contribution to the embroidery of the little house that graces the cover.

I want to express my sincere gratitude to Lisa Valdez, our first reader, who offered valuable observations. Her keen eyes and insightful comments were essential in shaping the foundations of this work, and I will always be deeply grateful to her.

My gratitude goes to Concepción "Connie" Sámano for her support and skill in style editing; not only did she improve the text, but she also provided clarity and coherence.

Similarly, I want to thank Lourdes Verónica Rodríguez Mandujano from the bottom of my heart for her meticulous review of the original manuscript in Spanish. Her dedication and diligence ensured that every word, every sentence, was carefully polished. Her tireless effort is a testament to her love for this project, and I owe her much more than words can express.

Finally, my deepest appreciation to Dr. Erin Gallo for her wonderful foreword, filled with insight and sensitivity. In her words, she embodies the ideals of Gayatri Spivak, who wisely asserts that the best readers and translators connect intimately with the text, developing a deep love for the stories it holds. Thank you, Erin, for conveying the emotional nuances of this work with such historical precision and elegance, bringing it close to the readers' hearts in such a beautiful and concise way.

Author's Note

The appointment is every Monday at one in the afternoon. With whom and what for? With my dear Jon Dell, and it's to edit my book. I'm enjoying every step, every revision, and I look forward to Mondays. Although the process has already been lengthened, I must remind myself that it is not easy to document my whole life. If it were, this book would have been published a long time ago. I think I have already memorized each chapter from so much reviewing. Even so, each time I always find something new to fix. Listening to the great writer, journalist, and commentator Juan Villoro (whom I admire a lot) mentions in one of his talks about another famous Mexican writer, Jorge Ibargüengoitia, who said that when reviewing before publishing one of his books, he realized that what took him more than two years to write would only take the reader a couple of hours to read, suddenly that's how I feel.

Someone else said, "publish it like it is because you're never going to say it's perfect."

I have been writing these pages for a very long time. I like to write poetry or prose, but I don't consider myself a writer, although I have several notebooks full of handwritten pages saved. Even so, I am intimidated when I read the books of the greats with their creative eloquence, their fascinating metaphors that sometimes I can't connect with reality because of their magical realism. But they insist (family and friends) "write your book, you have a lot of material, many anecdotes, your story is fascinating." Really? Are you encouraging me?

Little by little I began to believe it, so I started writing *desde la Navidad* [since Christmas]. "Since Christmas" is a saying that we use in the family when we want to know something more from the beginning, to get the whole picture. That is why when the idea arose to clarify a misunderstanding about my captivity in Texcoco, I decided to write to clarify any errors. The chapters were expanded backwards before I was born. It has been a real joy to form these lines to make a detailed account of what has happened to me, like Linda Ronstadt sings in the song *La cárcel de Cananea*.

Sometimes I despair, I want this project to be finished, so I can start another one I already have in mind, but I remember that I must enjoy the path to the hill before reaching the top. Take the time and inhale the scent of roses, admire the new day when I wake up and thank the Creator.

I have fun with my own jokes, or I get sad with my past disappointments. I am excited and thrilled to imagine the pleasure of future readers, especially my family.

This book is my legacy, a song to life in all its forms. Here I leave it to you, take the time to read it, as I took the time to live it and write it.

Chapter 1 – Twists of Fate

I'm a Chiapaneca, señores, of Lacandón origin—or at least, that's what this lovely song says (credit to my uncle, Eloy Esquinca). Well, maybe I'm not truly of Lacandón descent, but I am from that beautiful state of Chiapas.

We had to leave Chiapas and settle in another beautiful state of the Mexican Republic—none other than the State of Mexico, where I grew up.

By one of life's twists of fate, we ended up in Boyeros, a quaint little town nestled between the city and the pyramids, very close to Texcoco, cradle of our pre-Hispanic King Nezahualcóyotl.

We were forced to leave the southern lands behind—our home, our family. We can talk about it now; it's no longer a secret, and there's no danger anymore. You see, my father—they wanted to kill him.

In those regions, and in those times, killing or dying was an everyday thing. Whether it was a gathering, a celebration, or a local festivity—the reason didn't matter much. And according to what I heard my father say, all it took was a heated disagreement, a misunderstanding, or a grudge someone had been nursing, and *bam*! The pistols would come out and *órale*! Down went the dead man, and the tears came pouring.

Faster than you could blink, someone would pry a plank off their cart, grab another from a fence or a wall, and there they were—building the coffin to bury the poor soul. While the men hammered away, the widow's friends gathered to console her, and the neighborhood *lloronas* got the coffee ready, with a splash of tequila for the wake. There were always volunteers to bring the bread and tamales—because the party didn't stop, not even when the guest of honor was laid out in a wooden box.

But my father didn't stick around in Chiapas to celebrate his final farewell from inside a coffin, though they were already digging his grave.

He didn't want to leave his beloved land. He had his fields to work, his dairy cows, and his spirited, beautiful horse named *Cuando*, with whom he'd ridden through town, charming the girls. He was a real heartthrob—an expert rider, handsome and full of love to give. Ah, but in his own words, he didn't just take the girls—he courted them, sure—but when the time came, he'd marry properly, by the book, so as not to set a bad example.

So, the problem began with one of them. In Mexico, we say "*problema de faldas*": *faldas* [skirts] refers to women, and the phrase means problems with women. That is exactly why he had to leave his family and his country life on the ranch.

Before I was born, it so happened that my father married a beautiful young woman from the region. She came from a good family and had several brothers. Well, after the wedding festivities were over and the newlyweds were ready to head to their home, guess who went with them? The *suegrita*—the mother-in-law. And she didn't just stay for a day or two. Oh no. Two, three, four weeks went by, and finally, my father—already a bit annoyed—said to his new wife:

"Hey, that's enough! It's time for your mamacita to head back to her ranch. *Casados casa quieren*! Married folks need their own home! *Casa dos*, get it? We need our privacy!"

But the young woman, in all her arrogance, replied, "There are plenty of men out there, but only one mother. My *mami* is staying right here."

Well, no. That same afternoon, he packed up their things, loaded the cart, and sent the little wife with a case of *mamitis* and the mother-in-law with a bad case of *hijitis* right back to her parents' house. Back to her single-girl life they went—much to the shame of the family. Returning a newlywed bride was an insult that called for blood.

My father's life was in danger. The brothers, deeply offended by what they saw as an outrage, swore to take revenge to restore their sister's honor. *That insult would not go unanswered!*

But the years went by. The whole matter seemed forgotten. My father's enemies were quietly planning their revenge, but he just went on with his daily life. He had other girlfriends—until he met my mother! Their courtship was very romantic. My mom used to tell us how dazzled she was by that handsome man who came from another town, crossing rivers and mountains on his fine horse just to visit her.

After that sweet courtship, the outsider got very serious; and to show the young lady he had honorable intentions, he asked if he could bring his mother to formally ask for her hand in marriage. That's how serious he was!

As joyful as someone telling a fairy tale, my dear mother told us that when my grandmother showed up at the other grandmother's house to ask for the hand in marriage, the future mother-in-law came out with her measuring tape—right then and there, she took her measurements so she could sew the wedding dress herself! Now *that* was a real compliment!

She also told us that on the wedding day, they prepared dozens of stewed chickens, spicy pork, and all sorts of dishes I can't even remember. It was a grand, luxurious wedding!

Time went by. Everyone was happy, and to complete their joy, in the early hours of an October morning, I was born—lit by the most beautiful moon. That's where Miguel Michel's song *Luna de octubre* comes from.

Several lovely months passed. That pretty little girl with big eyes and curly hair—just like her papa—began taking her first steps. And mama was already pregnant with baby number two. They were eagerly hoping for a baby boy.

Do you remember those men who wanted to kill my father? Well, one afternoon, as my father was returning home from working the fields, a friend of his came up to him and warned him to be careful—four men, he said, had sworn revenge and were ready to strike. According to this friend, they were planning to invite him out—pretending they wanted to make peace. They'd take him to the cantina, get him drunk, and once he was good and gone, they'd help him onto his horse and, near the ravine, that's where they'd finish him off.

Thanks to that warning from the man—whose name, I now know, was Fidel—my father was able to prepare himself. And sure enough, they invited him to the tavern, tried to get him drunk. But my father, already aware of their wicked plan, pretended to drink the shots they kept handing to him. And when, according to them, he was good and drunk, they helped him out of the cantina and up onto his horse. Staggering just like a real drunk, he climbed on and started to gallop away.

Even now, my gut twists with fear at the thought that at any moment, the tragedy could have happened—and I might have been left an orphan without a father!

The men rode after their future victim, who looked so drunk he could barely stay upright on his horse. Then, feeling bold, they shouted, "*This is the end for you, Fulano Moreno!*"—just as they drew their weapons.

But faster than lightning, my father straightened up in the saddle—sober as ever—and, with a pistol in each hand... *pum, pum, pum, pum!* He shot all four of them dead and came out of it unharmed.

This really happened—I didn't see it in a movie. I'm not making it up. Honestly, they could make a great Netflix series out of these real events.

So off he went, still in shock over what had just happened, galloping away on his horse. He left the four bodies behind. He could have claimed it was self-defense—but he didn't. When he got home, he had to confess the deed to his mother, and surely to mine as well. Imagine the horror on both their faces.

The next day, he decided to go to work as usual. His mother begged him to hide, afraid that the cousins of the dead men would come looking for revenge and kill him right then and there. And—according to my father himself, when he would later tell us this story—he said, *"I'm not hiding anywhere. If they're looking for me, well, here I am!"*

That moment brings to mind the song La Valentina... *"If they're going to kill me tomorrow, they might as well kill me today."*

The next morning, just like any other day, he went out to work on the land. That's where his beloved sister found him—and I say, to this day, that he owes her his life. The youngest of my aunts.

With tears in her eyes and on her knees, my aunt Francisca—Quika—cried out, *"Because I love you so much, brother... I want you alive! Please, go. Just go!"*

Thanks to the desperate pleading of his youngest sister, my father finally agreed to leave behind his land and his family. Not long after, we followed—my mother, with her growing belly, and me.

He lived many more years and had many children and grandchildren, far from that southern land.

And that's how, instead of growing up in the beautiful state of Chiapas, my little siblings and I grew up in the also beautiful State of Mexico.

Chapter 2 – Humble Beginnings

We lived in borrowed homes for a while. First, we arrived at the house of one of my grandmother's brothers. My dad's uncle already had a full house, with a bunch of kids—my dad's cousins. I carry eternal gratitude in my heart for Uncle Carlitos and Aunt Agustinita: they opened their doors to give us shelter and food.

My father spent his days out looking for work, and my mother helped however she could, adjusting to life far from her family and homeland. It was so hard for her to watch her beloved husband come home tired and frustrated after doing whatever work he could find.

He even tried selling perfume door to door. My father used to tell us how awkward he felt pulling out a bottle so the lady of the house could smell it and decide whether to buy it, or not. That delicate work didn't suit him—so different from the rugged life of the countryside: preparing the land, planting, harvesting. *Oh, how he longed for those days!*

With a sad tone, my mother would tell us how it broke her heart to see her refined husband—the gallant man she had once met riding his proud horse *Cuando*, with all the elegance of a true gentleman—now down on his knees scrubbing floors. My sweet mother watched him with sorrow, because now he was doing the housework she used to help with. This time she couldn't—she was bedridden, recovering from a painful childbirth, cradling her newborn baby.

She also watched as her little girl, hungry, ate the leftovers of some oatmeal that my aunt had scraped into a tray. What my mother didn't know was that I was actually eating the best part of the breakfast. In Mexico, oatmeal *atole* is usually strained, and what's left in the strainer gets fed to the chickens. So, by eating what was meant for the hens, I was actually getting all the nutrients from the cereal. My mother didn't know that—and it filled her with sadness and helplessness.

Those first years went by. Eventually, my father found a steady job.

We moved to the little town where we would grow up. And it was all thanks to a *paisano* (compatriot) from Veracruz—because my father was originally from that state, on the Gulf of Mexico. This man, Don Chon, was building a house on the edge of town; the construction was already quite far along. It still needed a roof, windows, doors, and other finishing touches. My father suggested to his *paisano* that he let us build a small room there, just until he could find a plot of land to build our own home. That way, he'd be helping us out, and we could keep watch over the materials—cement, rebar, bricks, and all that—so they wouldn't get stolen.

So, happily, we moved into that tiny house: four walls and a cardboard roof, no electricity, no running water—but that wasn't a problem, because my father, never one to sit still, quickly dug us a well.

When we arrived in town, people looked at my mother as if she were a foreigner. Of course, the language was the same—but she spoke it like she was singing. Her long black hair was woven into two thick braids wrapped around her head like a crown. When she went to fetch water from a neighbor's house, she'd place the bucket on her head and walk tall, without spilling a single drop. She was so graceful... *la señora del llano*, that's what they started calling her. They gave her the name in part because the adobe house was surrounded by empty grassland which in Spanish is *llano*.

Chapter 3 – The Most Delicious Coffee

So much time had passed without seeing her family—her mother, her little sisters, her younger brother. The sadness filled her beautiful eyes. Finally, one day, my father, moved by compassion, said to her lovingly, *"Go see your family. It's not right that because of me, you can't visit them."*

My dear mother was overjoyed! She at once began preparing for the journey. Every day while making tortillas, she would set aside a ball of dough to make *totopos*. These *totopos* have a different texture, and the process is different too. I was around four years old, but I remember watching her make them thinner, and unlike tortillas, she wouldn't let them puff up on the third flip. She would poke little holes in them to let the steam out, and after the second turn, she'd stand them upright at the edge of the *comal* to toast slowly.

Little by little, she made ten in one day, fifteen the next, another batch the day after that—until she filled a sack with over a hundred *totopos*. That would be my father's food while we were away—probably with a little cheese. My father didn't know how to cook back then, although in later years, he would surprise us with his cooking skills.

For the trip, my mother sewed matching little dresses for my baby sister and me—adorable blue ones with tiny pink roses printed on them. I'm sure she prepared outfits for herself too.

The day of the trip finally came. They were both so nervous. It had to be a complete secret—they didn't want to leave any clue for my father's enemies. He had even changed his name, and the letters my mother wrote to her family were addressed to someone else, at an address in another country: Guatemala.

I once asked my mother why, at the beginning of her letters, she always wrote *Guatemala, Guatemala* before the date, and then began with *Querida mamacita…*

"*Ay, hijita,*" she told me mysteriously, "*it's to throw off the enemy.*"

Literally, it was to mislead anyone who might be looking for my father—just in case one of my mother's letters fell into the wrong hands, they would think we had gone to Guatemala.

My father took us to the train station. To me, everything was new and beautiful—I was so excited to climb aboard the train car.

I watched them say goodbye. I didn't understand why they were crying. It was a risk they were taking—for love. He, out of love for her, and she, out of love for her mother and her family in Chiapas.

After the train ride, we transferred to a bus, and when we got off, carrying a small trunk, we made our way toward the town. I was amazed when, from a distance, I saw my grandmother and my aunts running toward us, arms open, crying with joy. They reached her quickly and wrapped her in hugs, covering her face with kisses and tears. As we walked together, they helped carry her bags.

I, holding my little sister's hand, took in the Chiapaneco landscape and the delicious aroma of coffee drifting from the neighbors' homes.

Since then, I've believed that the most delicious coffee in the whole world comes from the state of Chiapas, in Mexico.

Chapter 4 – Our First Mansion

After an incredible month with our family in Chiapas, we returned to our little adobe house. We started adjusting to daily life in our new town. My mother didn't take long to make friends—everyone thought she was so lovely. Just hearing her speak with her Chiapaneco accent was like a lullaby.

She was also hilarious and full of sayings and stories. The neighbors were always entertained by her jokes and tall tales. I remember hearing her say once that a cat had fallen into our well—*and she'd point right to the corner of the yard, where the well was.* She'd mimic the cat's cries from deep down inside: *"miahogo, miahogo..."*—a clever play on *"me ahogo"* (I'm drowning) and the way cats meow in Spanish.

Then she'd say a turkey came waddling by, dragging its wings, calling out, *"cienpesosytesaco, cienpesosytesaco..."* ("a hundred pesos and I'll pull you out!"), mimicking the rushed, garbled sound turkeys make when they walk.

The women would already be in tears laughing—but my mom always delivered a punchline.

Next came a hen, clucking loudly: *"yasechingó, yasechingó..."* ("Too late now, you're screwed!")—and she'd imitate the sharp staccato of a hen's squawk.

Just imagine it— a chicken saying that! Oh, what fun we had!

Little by little, my mother became well-loved in the neighborhood. Several women wanted her to be their *comadre*. They took her to see the Catholic church, with all its saints. Back where she was from, there weren't any temples—of any denomination. She used to tell us that she said her prayers in the corner of the house, or under a bridge, or anywhere quiet and alone.

Before marrying my father, she had grown worried—she was almost 20 and had no suitor, let alone a fiancé. A few men had courted her, but she hadn't liked them and felt free to reject them. Wounded in their pride, those men began spreading rumors, trying to damage her reputation—saying she was no longer a virgin, that she was arrogant or unchaste.

To make matters worse, some dark spots started appearing on her lovely face—what people called *paño*. A bad omen for a young woman's reputation.

Distressed, she would go beneath that old bridge to pray and ask if the one meant to be her husband would arrive soon—someone who would restore her honor and treat her with respect. A prince from a faraway town.

And her prayers were answered. Not long after, my father arrived—riding his fine horse. As beautiful, she said, as the horse itself. That's how my mother always described him—with pride.

She also told us how serious my father's intentions were. After winning her heart, he promised he would bring his mother to formally ask for her hand. She prepared for that important day with great care, dressing in her best clothes. She went out to the field to pick flowers and— *oh!* — what pain! A bee, or maybe a wasp, stung her right on the face, leaving half her lovely features red and swollen.

Just imagine the surprise on the faces of the groom and future mother-in-law when they arrived and saw the bride-to-be's face all puffy! But it didn't stop the visit from happening.

My mother continued with her stories...

"*The wedding day,*" she'd say, "*was a grand event on your father's ranch.*" She showed us a photo from the day. The wedding dress, made by my grandmother, had a long train.

No one could have imagined that part of that very dress would one day be used to make me little dresses—since harder times were ahead, when they had to start over in new lands.

Now settled in the new town, the family grew—along with a good number of *compadres* and *comadres*, who were my godparents. We also gained kind neighbors who invited my mother to use their outdoor *lavaderos* to wash clothes.

It was hard work—pulling up water bucket by bucket from the well with a rope, to cook, wash dishes, bathe us kids, and who knows what else my mother managed to do with it. That's why, from time to time, she'd go wash clothes at a neighbor's house that had piped water and a real washbasin.

Oh, the houses the *ejidatarios* had! That's what they called the lucky ones who were there during the land grants. They were given a house *and* a piece of land to farm—an *ejido*. We arrived too late for that.

Apparently, back then, presidential candidate Manuel Ávila Camacho had promised that if he was elected, he'd reward folks with houses outfitted with electricity and indoor plumbing. You'd go inside to do your business, pull a lever, and *whoosh!* — everything would vanish down a magical pipe. And it didn't even smell!

As if that weren't enough, there was a shower, where water came out from above so you could bathe standing up—not sitting in a tub like we did.

What *we* got to enjoy was the little elementary school that bears his name: *Escuela Primaria Manuel Ávila Camacho*, where my siblings and I attended our first six years of school.

The ones who came too late, like us, had to find space on the outskirts and buy land however they could, to build a home. My father's *paisano* had a good-sized lot where he was building a big house. Many homes were still waiting for their cement roofs—a costly job—so they had to wait until they could save enough money for it.

Years passed. The family kept growing.

Yes, the family grew—but the little house did not. Just four walls, no windows, only a small skylight near the cardboard roof.

In one corner was my parents' bed where they slept with whichever newborn was "on rotation"—by then, there were two. In another corner was a crib that was a gift from my aunt for the youngest child—but my sister Lex and I slept there. Between the bed and crib was the sewing machine my grandmother gave my mother when I was born.

My mom was always busy—only stopping the pedal of the sewing machine when she was washing clothes or making tortillas. The only time she rested was when she was nursing the baby.

At night, that sewing machine became a nightstand, holding the candle that lit our room. That's also where we kept the alarm clock—if they didn't forget to wind it, it would keep ticking: *tick tock, tick tock*, its hands circling the numbers, telling us the time until it rang loudly at dawn to wake my father for work.

On one end of the hut was the little kerosene stove. On the other, there was a dish rack where my mom stored our few cooking utensils. Hanging on the wall by the stove was a wooden triangle my father made, with little nails to hang our mugs and spoons.

We also had a small table and a couple of chairs. Everything was neatly arranged.

My father brought home another bed—it was needed by then—but we had no room for it, so he hung it from the ceiling! Yes—from the beams that held up the cardboard sheets. It was really just a wooden frame, waiting for the day we'd have our own house and a mattress to go with it.

From the bed frame swung a little hammock, where my baby sister slept.

Outside, near the well my father had dug with a pick and shovel, he built us an outhouse that we called *el wáter*.

That was our very first mansion.

From the Source

Chapter 5 – Everyone but Me

One unforgettable day, my mother went to Doña Pancha's house with a basket full of dirty laundry to wash it at her tall *lavadero*, with piped water. I think it was a Saturday—a day we usually bathed—because my mother would always say, "*Sábado glorioso, te lavo, te baño, te plancho y te coso.*" ("*Glorious Saturday: I wash you, bathe you, iron and mend for you.*")

That day, she had left a big tub of water from the well out in the sun to warm up, so that when she returned, we could bathe. Normally, my sister and I would jump into the warm water together. But not the little boy—he was special. He had his own tub. So did the baby.

But that tub wouldn't be used for bathing—not that day.

While my mother was washing clothes at the kind neighbor's house, I, like other times, stayed behind to watch over my baby sister. She slept peacefully in her little hammock, unaware of the tragedy that was about to unfold.

The beans were boiling furiously in the pot. Suddenly, the flames on the little kerosene stove grew wild. They stretched and gained strength. I, a girl of barely six years old, had to make a quick decision: run to tell my mother—or try to stop the growing fire myself.

I turned off the stove, but the fire had already reached the wooden triangle where the spoons and mugs hung. Soon, the flames found their way up to the cardboard sheets of the roof.

There was no time to get my mother. No time to waste.

All I could think of was my baby sister—there, in her little bed, crying desperately from the heat of the flames. I don't know how I managed to climb up onto the sewing machine, reach the fragile hammock, pull her out, and with her in my arms, run out as fast as I could—to save us from the fire.

Neighbors came running from all directions with buckets, pails, and hoses. With enough water, they managed to put out the fire.

Someone went to tell my father that his house was burning. He arrived quickly, riding his bicycle, panick in his eyes.

I came out to meet him, holding my baby sister lovingly in my arms, beaming with pride at what I'd done—especially because the neighbors were hugging me, patting my back.

"What a brave little girl! Look how she saved her sister! How did she do it? She's so brave!" they said in admiration.

But my father didn't know that his eldest daughter had acted like a hero.

He was only worried about the house.

He jumped off his bicycle, distress in his eyes. Everyone watched him, concerned, unsure of what to say.

He looked at everyone—*everyone... except me.*

Chapter 6 – The First Stone

After the big scare, the little house had to be repaired. New cardboard sheets were needed for the roof.

Curiously, the bed hanging from the ceiling survived the flames—only part of the legs got scorched in the fire, but it was still intact when my dad took it down to check it.

That future bed, which at the time was just a wooden frame, went right back to its place up high. It looked like it was floating, but it was tied securely to the beams. Around the edges of the rectangular frame were grooves—not just for decoration, though they did look nice. They were made to hold the rope my dad wove across, first lengthwise, then across, threading it under and over until it was all laced tight, like a big stretched-out hammock. He did that when we were just about ready to leave that little house.

My father kept saving money and looking for a piece of land where we could build a house of our own. *It was getting urgent.*

And finally, one day, he came home smiling, full of joy, announcing that he had found a plot!

Out on the edge of town, toward the lake of Texcoco, where in the distance you could see the majestic *ahuehuetes*—those legendary, giant, leafy trees. Yes, that's where the long-awaited, if not exactly beautiful, piece of land was. Near the lot was a dreadful ravine, which people said was haunted during full-moon nights. (*Ay, how scary!*)

While my mother and father looked at it with hope in their eyes, I was honestly half terrified and disappointed.

But after the initial shock of seeing such a thorny, rocky patch of land where we were supposed to build our home, I began to get excited when my father, eyes gleaming with joy, said to me, "*You, hijita, are going to be my helper—my little worker. Tomorrow we start making adobe bricks!"*

How happy I was coming home from school, knowing my dad would soon arrive from work, and we'd head to the lot to make adobe bricks to build our own house.

I lost count of how many bricks we had. Every day, I'd ask, *"Is it almost time, papi? We have tons of adobe already!"*

"Not yet, mijita. It's still not enough."

Day after day, we kept at the task. I counted over a hundred bricks—but it still wasn't enough.

Then one day, my father decided it was time to start designing. He asked me for a piece of cardboard and a pencil to draw with. He walked back and forth across the land, stopping here, stepping there. That's how I remember my dad—completely focused on designing the house.

Finally, he drew the outline of what would become our home. When he chose where to start digging for the foundation, he picked up his pickaxe and shovel and began to hum a song. I watched, smiling, and sang along with him:
"Qué milagro chaparrita, ya hace días que no nos vemos... dentro de poquito tiempo por aquí nos miraremos, y si no, nos escribemos..."
(It's a song I've only ever heard him sing.)

The rectangle he dug into the ground was divided in two: one side would be the bedroom, the other the living-dining-kitchen area.

Laying the *first stone* is a solemn act—done with friends and *compadres*. Sometimes they toast with a shot of *pulque*.
"Congratulations, compadrito! Felicidades, compa! Let's get to work—first comes the hard part, then the hardest."

This was another level. From here, the expenses got even steeper.

Thankfully, my parents had been saving up.

The first stone.
The perfect angle.
The *cornerstone*—the one that would support the whole house. Everything depended on its strength.

A cross was raised at the center of the construction site, blessing the work. May 3rd is *Día de la Santa Cruz*, the *Day of the Holy Cross*—also known as *the day of the construction workers*.

As the solid walls rose—little by little, but faster than it took us to make the adobes—my job was to tuck little pieces of stone between each brick while the mud was still fresh. Yes, mud is also used to glue them together. Adobe on top of adobe, that's how the walls went up—tall and strong.

My dad said adding the little stones wasn't just decorative (though they did look pretty)—it gave the walls more strength. It all went so fast. I couldn't believe it when I saw the rooms already finished. Only the roof was missing.

This time, it wouldn't be made of cardboard sheets.

Chapter 7 – A Window for Mama

(A short play for three voices: Father, Daughter, and Narrator)

Narrator:
In a small town in Mexico, near the pyramids of Teotihuacán, a family from Chiapas is living in a borrowed house. Little by little, they begin building a home of their own on a rugged piece of land full of stones and thorns—*in a ravine where, they said, ghosts came out during full moons! ¡Ay, qué miedo!*

A young girl comes running home from school, thrilled that she'll get to help her father make adobe bricks to someday build their house.

Daughter:
Hi, Papi!

Father:
Hi, *mijita*.

Daughter:
Are we going to make adobe bricks now?

Father:
First you eat and do your homework.

Daughter:
No homework today, Papi!

Father:
Oh really? Then you can practice your lines—words with the letter "r." Sounds like you still haven't mastered them.

Daughter:
Okay, Papi. I *know* I haven't gotten them yet. Even my *mami* got frustrated and pulled my braids because I couldn't tell the difference between *río*, *ríe*, *rosa*, and *risa*!

(The little girl cries while saying the word "risa" [laughter], and her mother, moved by the irony, finally laughs at the oxymoron of her tears as the girl keeps crying and repeating: "risa... risa...")

Father:
Let's go now, hijita. Did you finish your lines?

Daughter:
Yes, Papi. Is the land where you bought the lot very far?

Father:
It's a little far. It's on the edge of town. There aren't many houses over there yet.

(Father and daughter walk a good distance. Dad stops and shows her a patch of rough, rocky land.)

Father:
Look, hijita—this is it. This is the land where we'll build our little house.

Daughter:
All *mami* wants is a big window, so she can look out in the mornings and say good morning to the sun.

Father:
Of course, *mi niña*! Our house will have a beautiful window!

Daughter:
But Papi, how are you going to build a house out of *nothing*? There's only dirt and rocks here.

Father:
Well, that's all we need for now. And with this shovel and this pickaxe, we'll get to work. Take this bucket and bring me some water from that little pond over there. It's not too deep—but be careful anyway. Wells are much deeper, but this pond is good enough to make adobes. I'll loosen the

dirt with my shovel and pick, dig a big hole, and with that loose earth and the water you bring, I'll make mud.

Daughter:
But Papi... why are you *dancing* on the mud? It looks like *mami's* brown tortilla dough!

Father:
No, *mi'ja*, I'm not dancing. I'm mixing the mud. Once the dirt and water are well mixed, we pour it into the wooden mold.

Daughter:
This mold that looks like two big rectangles—like giant cookie cutters, Papi?

Father:
Before we pour the mud into the mold, we have to mix in dry grass or straw. That helps it bind—it gives it strength. Ready?

Daughter:
Ready, Papi! Look, the adobes! You lift the mold and there they are—one pair, then another. Until you finish the mud. Then you make more!

Father:
That's right, *mijita*. And once they dry in the good sun, your job will be to flip them, so they dry on the other side too.

Daughter:
I love helping you, Papi. As soon as I get out of school, I run home and wait eagerly for you to arrive so we can make more bricks. I love watching you "dance" on the mud while I go get more water.

Father:
Look, *mi niña*—we already have more than a hundred adobe bricks! We'll be starting construction very soon!

Daughter:
Papi, don't forget to leave space for *mami's* window. Look, look—so many dry adobes now! I've got them lined up like little soldiers!

Father:
Yes, *mijita*. Soon we'll start raising the walls—but first, the foundation. I need to keep digging—straight, parallel lines to form the base of the house. With stones and cement we'll make the foundation. I'll have to make more mud to stack the adobes one on top of the other. So, my girl—bring more water from the pond!

Daughter:
It's amazing, Papi—how the walls are starting to form! I'm so excited, I can already see the shape of a house!

Father:
Look, *mi'ja*—in every corner we'll place pillars made of rebar and wire, then fill them with a mix of cement and gravel. That way, no wind will be strong enough to knock our house down!

Daughter:
And the roof, Papi? How will you make sure it doesn't fall on us while we're sleeping?

Father:
I've been saving, *hijita*, to buy the rebar. It's the most expensive part. They'll be woven across the top, then covered with cement and gravel. So strong, *mamita*, you could even stomp your feet and dance up there!

Daughter:
The window is so beautiful, Papi. *Mami's* going to love it. And now we'll be able to say: *Come into our house—it's yours. Mi casa es su casa.*

Chapter 8 – My Father's Surprise

Little by little, the new home began to take shape.

Meanwhile, back in the scorched little house, my sister Klelia gave up her title as the baby of the family and made way for the newest arrival: little Feliza. Now we were five—four sisters and one brother!

The ex-baby became really *chipil*—clingy and extra sensitive. She sniffled and cried over everything, even though Lex and I spoiled her with love and attention. She threw tantrums and could only be calmed with cuddles. If I didn't take her with me on errands, she'd throw herself on the floor crying. There was no choice but to give in.

Our routine looked like this: Lex and I went to school, my father worked in Chapingo and in the afternoons rushed to continue with the construction on our new house, and my mother cared for her "kindergarten" of little ones.

Sometimes, my dad would come home carrying white rolls tied up with rubber bands—like very important documents. He told us not to open them. *They were meant as a surprise, for when we moved into the new house,* which was almost ready. *Patience, patience.*

The mysterious rolls stayed stored beneath the bed. And more kept coming. We had to restrain our curiosity because we were very obedient. *He said not to open them— and we didn't!*

Then came the day we saw the walls of the new house fully built! All that was left was the final step: the roof—the biggest expense of all.

In our town, many houses stayed unfinished for years. Just shells. Just walls. Installing the roof requires lots of cement and steel rebar. And in every corner, you need those rods to build the pillars that hold up the roof—and added floors if you're building a multi-level house.

My father had taken out a loan (they called them *pensiones*) to buy the materials. That money was deducted little by little from his paycheck. Once he finished paying off one loan, he'd go for another.

When the loans were approved, he would go to the city and come back with a good sum in cash.

Feeling flush, he'd sometimes buy something special—like the time he arrived with a radio. Since we already had electricity, he plugged it into the wall, and suddenly we could hear music, news, radio dramas, and all kinds of commercials. It was on that *first Majestic radio* that we heard the terrible news: President Kennedy had been assassinated. My mother cried. We didn't even know who he was.

Another time, after getting a new loan, he brought home a new bicycle—which was soon stolen. Then he bought another one… and that one was stolen too.

One day, he came home with something delicious that we'd never tasted before: a big slab of *queso de puerco* (head cheese). It was already late when he arrived with this rare treat. Hearing him come in, we all got excited and jumped out of bed—even though we were supposed to be sleeping—and ate slice after slice.

My poor stomach, not used to so much fat, couldn't take it. After eating all that meat, I ended up vomiting until I nearly turned inside out. For many years, I couldn't even smell *queso de puerco* without getting nauseous.

This time, though, my dad didn't bring home any treats. All the money was for the materials to finish our home. Since it was risky to leave everything out in the open—especially in a house without doors—my father decided we'd sleep there, to protect the materials and not tempt any sticky-fingered neighbors.

We made a bed with cardboard and newspaper. We brought our pillows and blankets and slept under a sky full of stars, lit by the moon. *What beauty!* Who needed a roof when we had the most spectacular show from God's own creation?

The next morning, bright and early, friends, neighbors, and *compadres* arrived to help with the hardest and most expensive part of the construction.

By then, my father had already set up the pillars with the rebar—four in each corner, tied together with wire and wrapped in paper so the concrete mix wouldn't leak through. *"This is what will hold the house together. Even if there's an earthquake, it won't fall, mijita,"* he told me as he tied everything tightly.

On the roof, he had also woven a grid of rebar, crossing side to side. With the bags of cement, he'd already poured, everything was in place—just waiting for the *colado* (the concrete pour).

That's when the helpers got to work like little ants: some mixing cement, gravel, sand, and water; others hauling it in buckets to pour up top—and all of it had to be done fast, before the mix dried.

I watched the men move quickly. Some climbed ladders with full buckets while others handed down the empties to refill again. They poured concrete first into the pillars, then across the roof, until everything was covered—and then we waited for it to dry, praying it wouldn't rain.

"Ready Freddy!" they shouted, wiping sweat from their brows. Waiting for them was a well-earned feast: crispy pork tacos, handmade tortillas hot off the griddle, salsa ground in a *molcajete*, and a good, hearty drink of pulque. A fine reward.

All that was left now was the door and the window. My dad had left the right openings for them.

The door he installed—so strong, so solid—has lasted over half a century, opening and closing, blessing those who enter and those who leave.

And the window, just as my mother had dreamed, opened wide every morning to greet the gentle sun: *"Every morning the sun comes through my window, and I thank God for another day."* Juan Gabriel hadn't written that beautiful song yet, but it fits perfectly here.

The day of the move had arrived! My mother, holding her new little bundle in her arms, looked radiant. My sister Feliza had already arrived.

We brought our few belongings. We had (new to us) a gas stove, gifted by my aunt. I remember my mother still made tortillas over a wood fire. Next to the new house, my father built a separate kitchen with a proper hearth. We didn't have running water, so naturally, he dug another well.

That well also helped many of our neighbors. Whenever potable water was scarce, they came with buckets and pails to draw from it. It was amazing to see bucket after bucket fill—until eventually, only mud came up. *But the miracle came the next day!* Fresh water again—clean, cool, crystal clear. *(That well is still there, if you ever want to taste real water.)*

Our new house finally had space for the bed that had hung from the ceiling for so long. We laid it out, strung with rope, looped over and under, side to side—our makeshift mattress. The four of us fit across it: Lex and I on the edges, Lelis and Lichita in the middle.

That first night, I didn't go to sleep as quickly as everyone else. I stayed up helping my father unpack.

"Now, mijita," he said with joy, *"go get those rolls I've been saving for this day."*

Quicker than quick, I brought the box of long-protected treasures. I had no idea what they were.

With a hammer and nails in hand, my dad said, *"Hand me one."* My curiosity tingled as I picked up the first roll and opened it. My eyes widened in amazement: it was a very pretty woman with a very long neck.

"Look, Papi—a long-necked lady!"
"Yes, mijita—and there's more."

Next came another roll, which he nailed to the wall—this one, a beautiful landscape. It kept the long-necked lady company. Then another—another woman, just like the first. Then one with a girl and some chicks. And another—surprise! The same long-necked lady again.

Apparently, someone had sold or given my dad a bunch of calendars with the same picture. It didn't matter what year they were from—they weren't for the dates. They were to decorate our new *mansion*, which smelled of damp earth, fresh cement, and sunshine.

I noticed each poster had a name printed at the bottom. Since I already knew how to read, I leaned in and deciphered the letters. That's how I learned the name of that beautiful blonde woman with the regal neck: *Marilyn Monroe*.

The next morning, the family found the walls completely decorated with calendars in all kinds of designs—like an art show. Marilyn appeared over and over. My mother asked: *"And what's with all these faces of the same long-necked lady?"*

And so began the stories—now memories—in our home in Boyeros.

It still smelled brand new when my mother left once again... and returned with our baby sister Sary.

Two years later, those same walls welcomed little Lulú into the world.

Chapter 9 – We Didn't Know We Were Poor

We had plenty of space to run and play. We discovered that behind the house, we could mold the wet earth after the rain. It was soft and perfect for shaping little clay figurines. We made adorable miniature jars, tiny clay pots and pans—some deep enough for mole (a sauce made from chilis and sometimes chocolate, peanuts, and other ingredients), others flat for rice. Pots for beans and even pretend plates for serving imaginary meals.

Once our little dishes were formed, we'd take them to the kitchen where our mother was flipping tortillas on the *comal*. We'd set our creations beside the heat to dry. We were so happy. We didn't even know we were poor. We had no idea that toys were bought in stores, or that someone called Santa Claus existed. Nor did we have a television. We were free from commercials telling us to buy and consume.

Sometimes we'd go down a dusty trail to *allá abajo* [down there] to collect *tejocotes* (crab apples) and *capulines* (cherries) right where they took the cows out to graze. Or we'd go on a picnic to the *ahuehuetes*. There were no other houses nearby—we were the first to build in that area.

My mom planted *milpa* around the house. When the corn stalks started to droop from lack of rain, we watered them plant by plant—each of us with a little bucket—while I drew water from the well, down to the last drop, knowing that, miraculously, by the next day, the well would be full again.

My mother knew agricultural science—ancestral knowledge passed down through generations. With a shovel she'd dig the hole for planting corn. Next to it, she'd drop in a few beans or pumpkin seeds. When the corn grew tall, the bean vines would wind up the stalks, and the pods would dangle in the air instead of sprawling on the ground. It is much easier to pick them that way. The pumpkin plant, on the other hand, sprawled wherever it pleased—but finding pumpkins among the corn was never difficult. She also planted potatoes. At harvest time, we feasted on delicious, hearty vegetable stews. My mom used to say, *"Today I'm making you a delicious beef stew—without the beef."*

Little by little, neighbors moved into the area. First they built a house for Doña Salomé, sister-in-law of Maestra Sabina. Her house ended up closer to the ravine than ours.

From our house, we could still see the *ahuehuetes* in the distance—near the road where the passenger bus came into town twice a day. Once in the morning to take all the school kids to secondary school in Texcoco, and once in the afternoon to bring them back—along with townsfolk returning from errands or trips to the city for groceries.

My mom would spot the bus and say, *"Look, it's almost three—your dad will be here soon. The bus is my clock."*

One day, while we were enjoying our delicious pot beans with salsa—chopped chiles with onion and lime (*chilito con limón*)—and fresh tortillas hot off the *comal*, one of Doña Salomé's daughters arrived. She often came to sell maize.

"My mom wants to know if you'd like some quarts of corn," she said, standing in the doorway.

She stood there quietly, waiting for my mom's response. *"Yes, bring me two quarts,"* my mother said, savoring her meal. But the little girl didn't leave.

Then my mom tore a tortilla in half, dipped it in the bean broth, and handed it to the child. The girl took it gratefully and devoured it with delight.

Lex and I talked afterward—although we were enjoying a full plate of beans, the bite that had been given to that little girl somehow seemed more delicious than ours. So, we each took a tortilla, tore it in half, dipped it in the broth, and tried to recreate the moment. But somehow, we couldn't replicate the joy we'd seen in her face.

Maybe we needed to stand in the doorway and savor it before taking the bite.

The ravine behind the house—once said to be haunted during full moons—began to disappear. Houses were built there too. Big, fancy houses made of brick and block, not adobe like ours. There were two-story mansions... but ours wasn't any less than theirs.

My father even added a second story to our adobe house. That's why he'd left those steel rods sticking out from the corners—they served as future anchors for another level and (he always said) they also worked as lightning rods. So, during the great thunderstorms, with flashing lightning and crashing thunder, we never had to worry. We were protected.

More homes rose around ours. The town kept growing. Across the street from us, Don Lolo settled in. He had a large property and built a tall wall around it. On the other hand, he opened a general store where we got everything we needed. His wife, Doña Simonita, tended the shop.

We never carried cash. We paid on "credit"—meaning, a little notebook where she wrote down everything we owed. A liter of oil, a kilo of beans, some rice, some soap, and more.

At the end of every pay period, when my dad brought home his wages, my mom would go and make a payment. Just a *partial* one, because it was never enough to pay for everything. But unlike modern credit cards, Don Lolo and Doña Simonita didn't charge interest—they just added the remaining debt to the next month's tally. Without that little notebook, we wouldn't have eaten.

New neighbors kept arriving. Among them was Aurelia, daughter of Doña Paula and wife of "El Centavo." I never learned his real name—he was always known as *El Centavo* (The Penny), because he was short and scrawny. I don't recall him having sons, only daughters, and they were called *las Centavas*.

When Aurelia got married, she and her husband built one of those luxury homes, almost at the corner of town—right where the bus used to pass.

They blocked our view of the *ahuehuetes*, and we could no longer see the bus coming at three o'clock.

Aurelia and her husband came up with something new—they brought a giant loudspeaker that people could rent to play *Las Mañanitas* for their loved ones.

Suddenly, quiet dawns were shattered by full-volume birthday songs echoing across the town. Everyone knew whose birthday it was—because mostly the families who could afford it would blast it through the loudspeaker.

En la fresca y perfumada,
mañanita de tu santo,
recibe, mi bien amada,
la dulzura de mi canto.
Y encontrarás en tu mesa,
un fresco ramo de flores,
que mi corazón te deja,
chinita de mis amores...
Estas son las mañanitas...

Our neighborhood filled with people. The ravine transformed. And just like flowers in spring, tall, beautiful homes bloomed all around us.

Chapter 10 – My Tree and I

The floor in our new house was not dirt anymore. We no longer suffered from the fleas that would pop up from the ground and torment us with their bites.

We had the luxury of a polished floor. My dad could've been an engineer, an architect, a designer, or a plumber—and he was, all in one. It still amazes me how he built the house: he envisioned it and designed every corner, every space, and then came the floor. He used the same mixture he'd used for the roof and pillars, spreading it across the two rooms. He used a level to make sure everything came out even. Then, using a *llana* (a trowel), he smoothed it out until it was as flat and flawless as a sheet of paper.

When the surface was fully level but still wet, he added color to the mix. And then he did something more: using a ruler, he measured and marked squares of the same size to make the floor look like it was made of fancy mosaic tiles. Genius. Over 60 years later, that floor still holds its color.

In my memories, I can still see my dad crouched down, tools in hand, drawing the lines that would give our autumn-colored floor a look of elegance.

In the bedroom was the bed where my parents slept with the baby. Next to it was the crib—finally for my little brother Fidel. There was a big trunk where we kept important papers; I still wonder how they brought it all the way from Chiapas. It was as big as the crib. On the other side of the room, we placed the famous hanging bed, now woven with rope, side to side, which over time would wear down and break, but my dad would always mend it with more cords.

We still didn't have electricity, so my dad kept a candle close by to light our way. In the quiet of night, while we slept, you'd hear: "Papi, light the candle. I have to pee."

"Yes, hijita," he'd answer sleepily, striking a match to light the candle. We'd go outside to relieve ourselves, since we didn't have a bathroom indoors. We had a chamber pot instead. Sometimes he'd barely blown out the candle when we'd hear again: "Papi, light the candle. I have to pee."

I never once heard him complain or get angry. What patience he had!

Before bed, once we were all tucked under our blankets and sheets, we had to recite the bedtime prayer our mom taught us: "In the name of God and Holy Mary, amen. Good night, see you tomorrow, mamita." "Good night, daughter."

"Good night, see you tomorrow, papito." "Good night, daughter."

That was how we always said goodnight. One day, my mom thought the prayer was too short, so she added, "May God send us His blessing, amen."

So now we said "amen" *twice*: "In the name of God and Holy Mary, amen. May God send us His blessing, amen. Good night, see you tomorrow, mamita. Good night, see you tomorrow, papito." Remembering the repetition always makes me laugh.

Snuggled together in our long-awaited bed, the four sisters—Lex and I on either end. I had the idea of massaging our tired, battered feet after a long day without shoes. Once the candle was out, I'd whisper to Lex, "Pass me your foot." She'd gently pass it over our two sisters, sound asleep and unaware.

I'd start with the toes, giving each a rub and a satisfying pop—we called this part the "toe." Then came the "little hook," cleaning between each toe, getting out the grime and moisture from walking barefoot through dirt, puddles, and rocks. Next came the nails—we cleaned the gunk from around each one (what a delight!).

Then the rough, cracked heel, which I'd knead with strong hands. Then the ankle—a little pinch to the bone. Lex loved it. And most of all, she learned—because then it was my turn.

After the ankle came the calves, ending with the knees. I gave quick, firm massages. Lex took her time, slow and gentle. But she'd start to doze off, and I'd nudge her with my foot, so she'd keep going. "Here comes the other foot—you're not done yet!"

In our own made-up language, we called this nightly massage "foot."

Then, suddenly we'd hear my father's voice, "Be quiet! You're making such a racket. Go to sleep!"

That tradition stuck around. You could even bargain with it. "If you wash my dishes, I'll give you foot." Or, "Please kill that spider! How many foots do I get if I do it?"

Getting a foot was a true gift. And sometimes we'd beg for one: "Please, just give me foot."

Oh, what I'd give to have someone give me foot right now!

That's how the nights were in that bed full of girls. And come sunrise—time to rise and shine.

In this new house, we even had the luxury of two sinks: one for laundry and one for dishes, with a big basin in between, always full of water. Near the well, my dad built another basin—very handy, since we could pour water right in after drawing it.

And in front of those sinks, we watched a tree grow—one that my dad and I had planted together when it was just a little stick, just like in the song by Alberto Cortez.

There's even a picture of Lex and me with a swing hanging from one of its strong branches.

My Tree and I
Adapted from Alberto Cortez's poem, preserving the rhyme and warmth in English

My mother and I, we planted it—
There at the backyard's end,
Right where the house would finish up
And dreams would just begin.

It was my father who brought it home—
I was only five that day,
And what we planted in the ground
Was just a stick, some say.

Springtime came with sunshine bright,
We fed the earth with care,
We built a fence with wooden bits
To guard it growing there.

My tree took root.
My childhood flew.
And now beneath
Its branches true,
We share the memories—
My tree and I do.

Chapter 11 – Kaliman and Other Hard Truths

I don't remember exactly how much time passed before we finally had electricity. I'd go walking along the curbs behind our house and listen to songs I loved coming from the neighbors' radio like *Cielo Rojo* sung by Flor Silvestre. I also learned the song *Tú, sólo tú* with Pedro Infante—later made popular again by Linda Ronstadt on her album *Canciones de mi padre*.

So, when the day finally came and the poles were installed with all the wires running to each house in the new neighborhood, it was a huge celebration. We put away the candles. They installed light bulbs that, with a flick of a little switch, lit up the whole house—just like the sunrise.

My dad went to *pensiones* and brought home our very own radio. I was fascinated by the design of the brand name: *Majestic*. I'd trace the letters in the air with my finger, savoring the sound of each syllable: *ma, jes, tic*.

Now I didn't have to spend hours reading *The Thousand and One Nights*, even though it was exciting. It was way more fun to listen to shows on the electric box. Unfortunately, the bulbs inside kept burning out, and we didn't know how to replace them. We'd take it to Don Exiquio's son, who always had a pile of radios he was fixing. We had to wait our turn, which was agony when our favorite novela had left us hanging.

We waited anxiously for Mondays at 9:00 p.m.—that's when *La hora del Risámetro* aired, a comedy hour with three jokesters. One was El Indio Tepuja Régulo, another was Luis Pérez Vélez (I thought he was the funniest), and the third was Mister Kelly—who we called *Misterkely*. The three of them had us in stitches.

The audience would mail in jokes. Here's one El Indio Tepuja read: "A *compadre* was suing his *compadre* for stealing his little statue of the Virgin." The accused said to the judge, "*No, your honor, I didn't steal nothin' from my compadrito. When I was leavin' his house, I told him: 'Alrighty, compadrito, I'm off now. You stay here with God, and I'll take the Virgin.' I told him! That I was takin' her, and he didn't say nothin'. That's not stealin'—I warned him!*" That was the whole joke, and they'd play a laugh track over it. We believed it was a real live audience cracking up in the *Risámetro* studio.

Another show was *Apaga la luz y escucha*—Turn Off the Light and Listen—hosted by the chilling voice of Carlos López Moctezuma. It was full of horror stories, and even the music was scary. One tale was about a man walking at night who spotted a stunning woman. She waved him over and he followed her. She had her face covered by a veil, and her walk was so graceful he couldn't resist. Suddenly, he realized they were in a cemetery. She turned to face him— *and horror! It was Death!* (*La calaca tilica y flaca*)

During the day, adults listened to music on Radio L-Z. Songs like *El puente roto* with Irma Serrano, *Olvídate de todo menos de mí* by José Alfredo Jiménez sung by Lucha Villa, *El caballo blanco*, and other rancheras that bored me.

I'd ask permission to change the station. On Radio Mil and Radio Variedades, they played rock & roll: Angélica María, Rocío Dúrcal, Enrique Guzmán, César Costa, Manolo Muñoz, Palito Ortega, Alberto Vázquez, Leo Dan—all the big names. Recently, I was heartbroken to discover that many of those songs were just covers. Even *Eddy Eddy*, my favorite — *a cover!*

At school, the kids danced go-go. I learned the steps and danced by myself at home.

My mom listened to radionovelas while mending other people's pants. Neighbors brought her clothes to fix, and she'd work away on her sewing machine. She charged fifty or eighty centavos—never more than a peso. I think she charged too little. From old pants, she'd cut patches and sew them onto other pants, just a bit less worn.

We embroidered pillowcases and napkins while the novelas got dramatic. One was called *Entre mi amor y mi conciencia*, another was *Dicha prestada*.

Every day at 8:00 p.m. we listened to *Chucho el Roto*. When that novela ended, it was replaced by *Porfirio Cadena, El ojo de vidrio*—Porfirio the Glass Eye. In that one, the characters spoke with thick northern accents. Instead of *niño* or *chamaco*, they said *huerco*. *Pos* instead of *pues*. You'd hear galloping hooves and gunshots. Porfirio was always getting killed, but somehow in the next episode, he'd escape death—he always made it out alive.

Though fictional, the story was inspired by the real-life *Ojo de vidrio*, just like *Chucho el Roto*, the Mexican Robin Hood. Jesús Arriaga—his real name—was famous for faking his own death to escape from San Juan de Ulúa prison.

XEW's programming was fascinating and entertaining. We were glued to the radio.

But my all-time favorite, the one that completely captivated me—was the great Kalimán.

Gentleman with men, gallant with women, tender with children, ruthless with the wicked... such is Kalimán, the incredible man! He had a sidekick named Solín—who was secretly my boyfriend. No one knew.

In one episode, Kalimán traveled through the Lacandon jungle. He ventured into Bonampak. I was over the moon that my favorite hero was in Chiapas!

I was thrilled when they advertised a new weekly comic book with Kalimán. When the day so often announced on the radio finally came, I begged my mother for a peso to buy it. *"No!"* she said. *"We're not wasting money on that nonsense!"* But it wasn't nonsense—it was

Kalimán. He was special. *"I want to meet him!"* I pleaded. I couldn't convince her.

I wasn't the only one obsessed with him. At school, there was a group of kids just as crazy about him as I was. One day I saw them crowded around something—it was the comic! I rushed over. I craned my neck as far as I could. I was dying to see Kalimán. His voice on the radio was so powerful. The narrator would describe him: *"His piercing blue eyes, muscular body, and diamond-studded turban."* He was from India and spoke with a striking accent. A descendant of the goddess Kali. And now he was in a story I could *see*. I could see his face. And Solín's, too.

I'd seen other comics: Mafalda, Superman, El Payo, Chanoc, Archie and his friends. Also love-story weeklies like *Lágrimas y risas* and others like it. Those were just drawings someone had made.

I squeezed my way through the crowd of kids huddled around the lucky boy who had the money to buy the magazine. I was about to meet my hero! He flipped through the pages as we all looked on. I finally got close and saw him!

Oh... disappointment. My Kalimán and his little buddy Solín were just cartoons. Someone had drawn them. Not even in color.

Just like the Three Wise Men—Kalimán wasn't real. My heart broke. I was devastated.

But he went to Chiapas! It had to be true!

But no—it was all fiction.

I gathered the pieces of my shattered heart and went back to class.

Chapter 12 – "La tinguilica" and *My Make-Believe River*

This story took place in a spot that felt like a river. I don't know why I have such a fascination with rivers—so much so that I even wrote a song for the Willamette River here in Eugene.

In the town of Boyeros, where I grew up, there were no rivers or streams, just the half-dried lake of Texcoco. So, when the local *ejidatarios* dug enormous wells with large pipes to irrigate their plots of land, I imagined them as rivers.

On irrigation days, the women brought baskets of dirty laundry and found smooth stones shaped like washboards. There, in the large pools formed by the gushing water, they knelt to wash their clothes. The water would run down little ditches that the farmers dug, directing the precious liquid toward their crops—usually corn or alfalfa.

While the men irrigated, the women washed and chatted. The fields turned into a colorful patchwork of garments drying in the sun.

Those watering days brought back memories of Chiapas, where I was born. Down there, rivers abound—like the Usumacinta and the Suchiate. I remember my mom's joy when we visited Grandma Adulfa in the town of El Triunfo and then went on to Arriaga to visit Aunt Cirila. We all went swimming in the river. It felt like a party—my mom and her cousins were splashing and playing in the clear water.

Back in Boyeros, when word got out that the fields would be irrigated on a certain day, homemakers would gather their bundles of dirty clothes and either grab a bar of

Tepeyac soap or leave their laundry soaking in Roma detergent, ready to be rinsed in the cool waters.

There I was, among all the gossiping women, washing, rinsing, wringing out clothes. I preferred washing my little sisters' laundry over staying home scrubbing pots and pans, mopping the floors, or dealing with the crying and sniffles of the youngest ones. Oh, what a delight it was to wash with such an abundance of water—no need to pull it from the well or fill the tank! I looked forward to irrigation days.

One particular day is etched in my memory. I see myself playing with the water—pure bliss! Not only was I helping with chores, but I enjoyed it. I reveled in the touch of cool water and the magic of soap and hands scrubbing clothes. My sisters' once-grimy dresses now gleamed with cleanliness. *Bring me more clothes, bring me all the underwear— even Mom's and Dad's!*

Suddenly, the woman next to me playfully slapped the water, splashing my face. I laughed and did the same. I hit the water hard, and it splashed all over her head. She, with both hands, scooped more water and drenched me back. I returned the favor. But then she got angry, grabbed me by the hair, yelling and insulting me.

"You insolent little brat! Look how you soaked me! Now I'll give you a real bath," she shouted, shoving me into the pool, dunking my head again and again. I was crying.

I don't remember how long it lasted. I can't explain why none of the other women stepped in—maybe they were enjoying the show. All I remember is suddenly seeing my mother charging toward us, furious.

"Who's the witch that laid hands on my daughter? How dare you? Pick on someone your own size, you miserable woman!" she shouted, yanking the woman by the hair and slapping her. "How dare you abuse a child, you wretched witch!" Then she looked at me and barked, "Grab your rags! We're leaving."

"You're never coming back here to wash with this bunch! We have a perfectly good washbasin your father built."

Now, looking back, I wonder—how did my mom get there so fast?

Talking about it with my little sister Klelia—the one who followed me everywhere—she remembered that when she saw me being dunked and dragged, she ran straight home, where our mom was making tortillas. Mom pulled them right off the *comal*, and with her apron still on, didn't just run—she flew, ready to show the world what a mother does when someone harms her child.

Turns out, the abusive woman had the same name as me: Margarita. So, my mom decided that such a pretty name wasn't fit for her. From then on, she called her *La Tinguilica*.

From Boyeros to Chapingo, we had to pass by La Tinguilica's house. Yes, I'd get nervous walking by, but honestly, I think she was more afraid of us. She never even peeked her nose out when we passed.

Ah, memories...

Though I'll admit—I did miss washing clothes at my make-believe river.

Chapter 13 – School Days, Cruel Days

My little sister Lex and I would take the passenger bus to the ESFIR—Escuela Secundaria Federal Ignacio Ramírez. To get in, you had to pass an entrance exam. My father exhorted (more like threatened) me with the idea that if I didn't pass it, he'd make me go work as a housekeeper for Teacher Sabina. It wouldn't have been degrading to work with her, but the way he said it—so harsh and humiliating—it felt like a punishment.

When I found out I'd passed that exam, I jumped for joy. I was ecstatic! I felt like a whole new person. A whole new world opened before me. *Goodbye cruel world!* I shouted, I sang!

Oh, goodbye cruel world, I'll never see you again. I'll say I never knew you—but everyone will understand... how marvelous it is to leave this cruel world...—sung by Enrique Guzmán.

See, the kids in elementary school had been cruel—*extremely* cruel. They gave me the most ridiculous nicknames. Today, we'd call it bullying, *even in Spanish*. I lived it. One kid would shove me, another would jab me with a pencil, another would scribble in my notebook. I'd ask for help. "Teacher, look at what he's doing... Teacher, he pulled my braids... Teacher..." They mocked me, saying I was a tattletale, always calling "Teacher... Teacher..."

They said I should be called *Tabloide*, after the gossip newspaper of that time.

Every day was torment.

One day, I had the big idea to bring a little doll my aunt had given me. Bad idea. They snatched it away and tossed it back and forth like a ball. I cried and begged, "Please give me back my dolly!" Poor thing ended up like me—hair all messed up.

There was a time we were going on a field trip to the Teotihuacán pyramids. The fee was seven pesos. But I misunderstood and told my mom it was *seven hundred*. She was shocked and went to ask the teacher why it was so expensive. The problem was—she asked in front of the whole class. The little monsters burst out laughing, and from then on they called me *La Zetezientos Pesos*, mocking not only my mistake but also my lisp.

Anything was reason enough for them to assign me a new nickname. They made fun of my eyes, saying they were huge like a bull's—*Ojos de toro loco*. Another name on the long list.

They were awful. I hated them with all my heart. But what could I do? I was a coward. I didn't know how to defend myself. Not like my sister Clelia. She'd fight tooth and nail. But not me. I'd tremble. I never fought back. And I didn't tell my mom. What for? The whole *zetezientos pesos* mess was already enough.

One of those awful boys lived way down the road—not near the *tejocotes*, but heading toward the *ahuehuetes*, if you walked straight. That villain—brother to María Luisa (she wasn't mean)—one day, out of nowhere, punched me in the back. I turned around, shocked and in pain. He sneered, "You'll live."

I stared at him, helpless and furious. In my head, I begged God: "Punish him! Please, God, give him nightmares! Make him have awful dreams! Don't let this go unpunished! Punish him—I can't!"

Years later, I saw him again. I didn't recognize him—but he recognized me.

"You look great," he said, charming. "Looks like life's treated you well."

Once I really looked at him—I knew. He tried to make small talk, the worm! I remembered that moment in grade school. I only nodded, silently thinking: *Yes, I'm doing great. Look at me. I've seen the world. I've grown wings. I'm just visiting, and you're still stuck in the same corner. You creep.*

I don't hold a grudge. My heart has no room for pettiness. But I do remember.

I must be a bit of a masochist. Here I am, remembering how miserable I was at school. I'm not the first or the last to suffer that kind of abuse. I just hope someone reading this finds some clarity, some strength to help others or stop this from happening.

Here's another one:

My dad bought me a mechanical pencil—such a beautiful one! Orange, but see-through. You could see the leads inside. No sharpening needed! And it came from my dad—he *never* bought me anything. I was so proud of it. I left it on my desk. Looked down to grab my notebook and when I looked back—gone.

I panicked, looked all around. Everyone looked innocent.

"Who took my pencil? Please give it back! Don't be mean—please!" I cried, tears soaking my blouse.

"Stop crying," said Chimbombo, mocking me. "Save your tears for when your dad punishes you for losing your precious pencil."

In the middle of that hell, God sent me an angel: my beautiful teacher—Amparo. Her name means protection, and she lived up to it. She even defended me from her own son Jorge, who was also awful to me.

She moved my desk away from the others, to the far corner, away from the troublesome students. But that only made me an easier target. The boys would shoot orange peels at me with rubber bands. Those hits hurt.

One day, Miss Amparo gave me movie tickets. "For your dedication and effort," she said. Looking back, I think she just wanted to do something nice for me.

She even planned ahead. "These brats will try to take your tickets," she warned. "I'll let you out an hour early—run home and enjoy your reward."

I'll never forget her kind deed. We went to Texcoco and saw *Ahí está el detalle* with Cantinflas. I'd never been to the movies before.

It would've been perfect to have Miss Amparo the following year, but in sixth grade, I had a new teacher—Mr. Valverde. For the Mother's Day program in May, he asked me to stay after school to rehearse a poem. I told my mom I'd be late.

One of those afternoons, after rehearsal, he called me to his desk. He pulled me close and hugged me—and kissed me.

I felt faint with fear. But he was kind to me, and after all the cruelty from the kids, it felt comforting to be treated gently. Still, I was very nervous being alone with him.

Then during one recess, I overheard some older girls talking: "Did you know you can get pregnant just from a kiss?" one of them said.

I panicked. I *had* to tell my mom.

"Maestro Valverde kissed me," I said. "Maybe I'm pregnant!"

She wiped her hands—she'd been washing diapers—and we went straight to the school. The teacher was alone in the classroom. I didn't go in. I waited outside. I don't know what she said, or what he replied, but his attitude changed completely.

No more kindness.

By the end of the school year—he flunked me. I had to repeat sixth grade.

What an injustice. What shame. Failing a grade was for slackers. But I was doing fine in all my classes. *Damn you, Valverde!*

I repeated the year with another teacher. Valverde didn't return. Thank goodness.

People said the new teacher wasn't even a real teacher—they'd seen her selling vegetables at the market. I wouldn't have cared if she'd taught well. But she didn't. She brought her girlfriends to class and spent the whole time gossiping. Meanwhile, we had to copy things over and over.

One day she told us to write a poem while she chatted with her friend. I was thrilled. I love writing. Rhyme came naturally to me. My mom, God, nature—those were my muses. I could've written about love, but I was too shy. So, I wrote verses like this:

Mamita, mamita, forgive me please,
for talking back yesterday.
I love you with all my heart,
I won't do it again today.

I gave that little poem to my mom with a wildflower bouquet. I remember how her face softened—usually so tired and worn. Her tender green eyes welled with tears, and she hugged me.

I was so inspired, happily scribbling away when—not the teacher, but her friend—walked by, glanced at my notebook, and yelled: "You didn't write this. Teacher said to write, not to copy. Erase it and write something original."

I couldn't argue. What was the point? I buried my hurt, my shame, my rage and told myself: *So, this is why I repeated the year? Hang in there—it'll be over soon.*

And finally, that seven-year nightmare of primary school was behind me. I became a secondary school student.

A year later, my sister Lex passed the ESFIR entrance exam too. That next school year would be the happiest of my life—with her by my side.

Chapter 14 – The Price of the Ride

The fare for the passenger bus back then was thirty centavos; as students, we paid half—just fifteen centavos! Every morning, my little sister and I would grab our schoolbags with our books and notebooks, our delicious tacos for lunch, and our thirty centavos. She wore her pink uniform for first-year students, and I wore my blue one for second year of middle school. They were beautiful jumpers, each with a white blouse underneath. That same blouse could be used for P.E. day, paired with a blue skirt trimmed with three white bias-tape stripes, plus white shorts and white sneakers.

To buy those uniforms, my mother sold one of the piglets she had been fattening up for just such expenses. On the edge of our property, we had a *chiquero*. That's what we called the pigpen, where the pigs—also known as *puercos* or *cerdos*—were fed with all the food scraps. They got so excited when we brought them the starchy water (*achihual*) from where my mom washed her hands while making tortillas. I loved the noisy sounds they made, chewing their food with such gusto. We gave them corn husks and even the cleaned corn cobs after we had picked the kernels off. They ate it all up, noisily and messily.

The sow gave birth to her piglets. So cute, squealing and nursing all over their lying-down mother, each one piling up, each clinging to a teat.

We also had chickens, turkeys, and ducks. (And mice, though those weren't good for anything.) Sometimes the baby turkeys would get chickenpox-like pustules. They'd walk around with swollen bumps on their little heads, sometimes so close to their eyes that they couldn't see, bumping into each other pitifully. My mom would treat them—she didn't know about vaccines or didn't want to spend the money. She'd pluck a feather from a rooster or hen, dip the tip into fresh chicken poop (more liquid and purplish than turkey droppings), and dab it on the bird's bumps. Once it dried, the pustules would fall off. A holy remedy! That baby bird would grow up just fine, well-fed with cracked corn and powdered alfalfa, ready to be the star of some future birthday feast.

The piglets were for sale. We never ate one ourselves.

Thanks to the sale of those piglets, we got brand-new shoes. The days of walking to school in shoes so worn out that they flapped open in front like little mouths—exposing toes like teeth—were behind us. People would joke, "Your shoes are hungry!" One day my sister said, "I'd rather go barefoot," because the flapping made walking uncomfortable. But I preferred wearing my starving shoes over going barefoot to school.

Every Monday, we had flag-raising ceremonies. Our mom coached us for school poems about heroes, mothers, the flag, springtime, and other things. She taught us how to use our voices, our hands, our posture. My sister was more graceful than I was when reciting. The teachers didn't need to do a thing—our mom took care of it all. The school even won poetry contests between districts.

That Monday, the teacher told my sister she was up to recite a poem to the flag. "Of course!" said my mom. "You know what to do. Graceful and with good memory." She dressed her up in her best little dress, combed her hair with lemon juice to slick it down, and braided it into two thick plaits with white bows. And since we didn't have shoes for her, my mom cleaned her little feet, rubbed them with moisturizer, and polished them until they gleamed. Everything looked great—except I was embarrassed she had to go barefoot.

When we got back from school, my mom asked excitedly, "How did your sister do reciting?"

I said, "Terrible, because she was barefoot."

"Oh, you're useless," she snapped. "I didn't ask how she looked—I asked how she recited!"

Well then. I got scolded *again*—she even gave me a *sape* (a smack on the head) and sent me off to wash dishes.

But that was in the past. Now, we rode the bus happily toward our middle school. Sometimes we got out early and waited at the bus station for two hours until the next departure. Then we'd exchange mischievous glances and say in unison: "Wanna walk?"

"Let's do it!"
"¡Órale, vámonos!"

The route was simple. The little bus left Texcoco, passed through San Felipe on its way to the nearby town of Boyeros, turned around by the *ahuehuetes* (big cypress trees), and then back again. We didn't need to go all the way to the *ahuehuetes*. We could take a shortcut—crossing the dry riverbed, cutting through cornfields and alfalfa patches—and still beat the bus home.

Sure, the trek across dusty, rocky roads and through San Felipe was tough, but we were so happy. This memory still fills us with joy. I can still see those little girls, hand in hand, walking without a care in the world.

Ah, but we didn't want to ruin our nice new shoes on those rocky paths. So, we took them off and walked barefoot. As a reward, we could spend fifteen centavos of our bus fare on candy!

"Should we stop and buy something?" we'd ask each other in a sing-song voice.

"Yes!" we'd shout and hop with glee.

There was a little shop on the edge of San Felipe, right before we crossed the dry river. There, we treated ourselves: bubble gum balls, banana-flavored *Motita* gum, *pirulines*, candies shaped like peanuts, and others that looked like little clocks. (I haven't seen those candies in years.) Our fifteen centavos went a long way. Sometimes we'd arrive home before the bus, sometimes right after it—but always with a piece of candy to give our mom, fifteen centavos to return, and our shoes: spotless, shiny, and untouched.

Chapter 15 – Glorious Saturday

Every Saturday—rain or shine, whether we needed it or not—it was bath day. In a big metal pot, placed over burning logs, we heated water. My mom would pour it into a large round tub, and all of us girls, my little sisters and I, would pile in altogether. We scrubbed each other's feet, which were always the dirtiest part of us after going barefoot all day long. Dirt built up around our ankles. Our skin darkened from cinnamon to chocolate. Our elbows, knees, and even our necks looked grimy—but we didn't scrub those with the pumice stone. The feet, though, needed a full-on scrubbing: pumice stone, rough sponge, and plenty of soap. Our cracked heels, worn from jumping around without shoes, ended up soft and smooth after a good soak. Then my mom would lather our hair with Tepeyac soap and rinse us off with a bucket of clean water.

We came out clean and glowing—at least until the next Saturday. So, I really didn't understand what happened that one day at school, back in elementary school. We were lined up in our rows, ready to go into the classrooms, when a teacher got the bright idea to send her favorite student to inspect everyone's ears to see if they were clean.

There I was, standing in my fifth- or sixth-grade line—I can't remember exactly—and I saw the chosen student coming. A very proper girl named Ena (a name derived from the initials of the National School of Agriculture, where her father worked in Chapingo). She was fair-skinned and rosy, peach-like, and very graceful. Of course, the teacher picked her; she was so clean and pretty. The teacher probably wished we all looked like Ena.

As I watched her approach, I felt confident. We bathed every Saturday, after all. I had nothing to worry about. Ena seemed to be enjoying the task. She stopped in front of each student, checked inside and behind their ears, then moved on. She came up to me, examined me, and then—unbelievably—raised her finger to point and said: "Her ears are dirty!"

What?! Me?!
Earth, swallow me now.
What a shame!
How could this happen?
She must've made a mistake.
She didn't look properly!

I ran home with the humiliation heavy on my back, unable to believe my ears—pun intended.
"Mami, mami! Can you believe the teacher sent Ena to check everyone's ears? And she said mine were dirty! She sent me home to bathe!"

"It's okay, sweetie. Tomorrow's Saturday, it's bath day anyway, and you'll wash them well," said my mom calmly.
"And it's a good thing they sent you home. I've got a pile of diapers to wash."

Ah, *la Ena.* Note the use of *la* before a proper name—that's how we expressed annoyance in the place where I grew up. Even though I know Ena was just following orders, I still carried that feeling of irritation for the shame she caused me. Ironically, she had a crush on César, a handsome boy who was the son of Doña Socorro. But the one chasing her was a rather unattractive guy named Memo, Régula's brother. That beautiful, refined, clean Ena ended up marrying Memo. So now she can check *his* greasy, unattractive ears!

By the time we were in middle school, we looked quite cute in our uniforms. Though I think we still only bathed on Saturdays. My mom's motto was always: "Glorious Saturday: I bathe you, I wash you, I iron you, and I sew you." So that day we also washed our uniforms.

One Wednesday, I found it strange to see my friend Alma Rosa Perdigón, a lovely girl from a wealthy family, washing her white blouse. She was scrubbing the collar over and over again. "It's just so dirty," she said. It didn't occur to me to look at my own. I'm sure it was filthy too. Good thing Ena wasn't at ESFIR to check collars—she probably would've sent me home again.

But my mom didn't say anything. She was too busy with so many little ones to worry much about our appearance. My blue jumper was super tight. I felt like a tamal in its husk. My body was changing. The jumper didn't even have room in the bust—it was shaped like a pillowcase. Thankfully, Aunt Agustinita visited and brought me my cousin Olga's second-year uniform. She was in third year now, and her jumper was burgundy.

My mom also didn't see the need to buy me a bra. The first one I ever had was an unexpected gift—very fancy, and it fit me perfectly. But I didn't enjoy it for long.

Around that time, a beautiful sister of my dad's arrived—with many daughters, each with a different last name. She wasn't visiting. She came to stay. My pretty cousins brought lice with them. We all caught them. Soon, we were infested. But that wasn't the worst of it.

My aunt would go out in the afternoons, all perfumed and dolled up like a porcelain doll, always taking her oldest daughter with her. One afternoon she told my mom, "Look, sweetheart, you're not bad-looking at all. You're poor because you want to be. You could go out with me one evening and come home with your own little money."

That same day, my dad threw her out: "You shameless tramp! I opened the doors of my home to you, and you bring this... filth into it." (Though he used a harsher word.)

She had to leave with all her little girls.

Later, she would come back to visit and bring us clothes that people gave her. That's when I found that lovely little lace bra. It fit like a dream. Since we didn't have a mirror, I'd sneak a peek at myself in the water trough. I loved how I looked. I hid the bra under the mattress so no one would find it and wore it secretly. I was so modest and shy.

One day, my dad came home half-drunk. My aunt happened to be visiting. He insulted her and kicked her out again. She yelled back, "Oh, but you're all so quick to wear the clothes I bring you, huh?"

"What clothes?" he demanded.

"I don't want anything from this witch," he roared. "She could have cursed it all! Throw out everything she's given you, and I'll burn it here and now. I'll set fire to all of it!"

"Everything!" he shouted. "Did you hear me? EVERYTHING!"

I still can't believe how obedient we were. I couldn't even hide that beautiful bra... because he said *everything*.

Chapter 16 – Sweet Bread and Little Sins

Let me tell you about my First Communion dress. This story has bittersweet shades, though sweeter than bitter. The dress was very simple and austere. No lace, ruffles, or crinoline like the other girls' dresses.

My godmother Lala offered to buy me the entire outfit. What would it have cost my mom to let her? But no. "No, comadrita, don't worry. I'll make her little dress myself. And don't bother with the shoes either—Tía Agustinita already gave us a pair."

A few months earlier, my aunt had brought us some *huge* shoes, probably size eight (I think they would've fit my dad). To make things worse, they didn't have buckles. They looked like canoes. My mom appreciated them very much. She thanked my aunt and, as soon as she left, cleaned them up, painted them white with a polish called *Apresto*, and set them neatly against the wall to dry. "Don't even think about wearing them," she warned me. "They're for your First Communion."

I thought to myself: Who *would* want to wear them? They're hideous—and enormous. Maybe my feet will grow from now till December? Hopefully, because if not, they'll be flopping off with every step. And that's exactly what happened: my little Cinderella foot stayed small, and the shoes still looked like gondolas from Xochimilco.

My mom made the dress out of a soft white silk. It honestly looked more like a slip than a dress. If only she'd added a little bit of tulle on top—was that too expensive? She did at least sew a tiny lace trim onto the chest of the blouse, so it looked somewhat like a dress and not a nightgown.

On the eve of the big day—December 11th—the town priest arrived at the parish, and everyone about to make their First Communion had to go to confession. It was urgent for me to confess, because there was a *mortal sin* weighing heavily on my conscience.

When it was my turn, I knelt in front of the confessional.

"Hail Mary Most Pure," came the priest's voice from the other side.

"Conceived without sin, Father," I replied.

"Tell me your sins, child."

"Oh, Father, I can't carry this guilt anymore. See, my little sister was eating her *bolillo* roll. And I wanted it so badly, I just couldn't resist. You see, Father, in our house we only get tortillas. The bread is for the little ones, supposedly because it has more nutrients. But I wanted it *so* bad! So, I made sure no one was watching, and I took a little bite of her *bolillo*. But…"

"But what, daughter?" the priest asked, surely holding back laughter.

"Well… I bit her finger, Father! Just a little, by accident! My little sister cried a bit, but then she got over it and no one found out. Just me. But I *know* God was watching me."

"Your sins are forgiven, child. Go and pray twenty Hail Marys and twenty Our Fathers. And behave yourself."

"Oh, thank you, Father!" What a relief—I had lifted the weight of my guilt!

As I headed off to pray, I saw the line of girls waiting to confess. There was one of the *Centavas*—yes, one of them. I couldn't believe what I was seeing: she made bunny nose twitches at me and stuck out her tongue! What a little brat! Surely she had some confessing to do too. I pretended not to see her. I couldn't risk sinning, even in thought.

When I got home, my mom shut me away—well, more like tucked me behind the bed. I wasn't allowed to come out, so I wouldn't be tempted to argue or pick fights with my siblings. I couldn't eat either. I had to fast until I received my First Communion the next day.

On December 12th, I bathed early. My mom carefully rubbed lemon juice into my rebellious curls. It worked wonders. She helped me dress in the night-gown, I mean, dress. My godmother showed up with some curious items: a little lace purse (a *limosnera*), a decorated white candle, a tiny Bible, and a veil like a miniature wedding veil. And since her father was a baker, my madrina Lala arrived with a giant basket of sweet breads—every kind I could ever dream of: *conchas, besos, huaraches, tabiques, novias, polvorones, hojaldras, niños envueltos, piedras, pambazos, cuernitos, donas, flautas, biscochos, bolillos, teleras, ojos de pancha, cocoles*. Was I dreaming? Had the fasting made me hallucinate?

"Come on, hija, let's go to your First Communion, and when we come back you can eat all the sweet bread you want," my godmother said in a rush.

That was a happy day. It didn't matter that my dress was so plain, while the other girls looked like princesses. Or that my gondola-shoes slipped off with every step. After receiving the Holy Host, a rainbow of sweet bread awaited me. (*Panderuza*, as my grandson Antonio Jared Gilson would say half a century later, thinking "pan de dulce" sounded like *panderuza* in English.)

Chapter 17 – The ignored *quinceañera*

My mother was resourceful—in other words, a genius. That saying, "If life gives you lemons, make lemonade," could've been written just for her, because she knew how to make the most of what she had. We were amazed by what she did with a whole sack of ties. Yes, ties! Student ties. At that time, the University of Chapingo (the National School of Agriculture, or ENA) was still militarized. The young men wore a khaki uniform: trousers, shirts, ties, and caps. When they went home for vacation, they left behind whatever they didn't need —ties and caps, mostly. A lot of those items ended up in the trash.

So, my dad, knowing how industrious his dear wife was, brought them home. We all stared at him with puzzled expressions— "What on earth are we supposed to do with all these beige ties?"—but before we knew it, we were all unpicking seams, and my mom was at her sewing machine, stitching the strips together into fabric. She alternated the direction of the ties—one up, one down—creating rectangles that she then joined into a thick, sturdy quilt (in a lovely "dirt" color). That night, we slept warmly under our brand-new bedcover.

Yes, my mom worked miracles. Even though she never studied tailoring or design, she sewed our clothes. For my sixth-grade graduation, the moms' committee picked a dress pattern from a fashion magazine: a light blue satin dress with a pleated front and fancy lace trim called *guipure*. We were also supposed to wear a little headpiece. When my mom saw the magazine, she said, "I'm not going to spend money on a seamstress—I can do that." She went to the market to buy the fabric and the so-called *guipure*.

Despite her best efforts, the pleats on the front of the dress came out looking more like a giant pouch across my chest. The headpiece? It looked like a burst of light exploding out of my head. I still have the photo. The worst part was the teasing from the other girls with dresses sewn by a famous local dressmaker.

But it didn't matter. I was graduating and heading off to secondary school!

As my fifteenth birthday approached, my aunt Virginia offered to make my *quinceañera* dress. I'm not sure she had any formal training in sewing either.

She wasn't my mom's sister—she was her sister-in-law, married to my uncle Jesús. They came to visit our little town unexpectedly, and what a surprise! We had never met him. My mom had several half-siblings, since my grandfather José Vicente was quite the wretch. Uncle Jesús had heard about his little sister and came looking for her. He brought along his girlfriend, a beautiful woman dressed in the latest '60s fashion—poofy skirts, crinolines, the works.

He would say to us, gazing at her lovingly, "Go on, tell her, *tía*." They got married and started visiting us in their car. We thought they were rich—after all, they lived in the city and owned a car!

On their next visit, they brought a beautiful baby girl: pale, rosy, and delicate like a flower. We paraded her around the village— "Look, this is our little cousin. Isn't she pretty? My aunt and uncle have a car!" (Nobody was even asking.)

Then came another cousin, and another. The family kept growing.

Eventually, my aunt needed help. During school vacations, I'd go stay with her in the city to lend a hand with the kids. Life there was completely different. Instead of waking up to roosters crowing or pigs squealing for their corn or chickens clucking in the coop, or dogs barking in the yard, I was woken by the roar of car engines on the early morning streets of Mexico City. What a thrill—I was in the city!

I loved being with my aunt and uncle—their conversations, the piano, the ham-and-egg breakfasts. When my cousin turned one, they threw a fabulous party. There was music from La Sonora Santanera with my uncle playing the piano and other musicians playing fun hits like *La Boa*— "those sitting know it, those dancing know it." Everyone was eating, drinking, dancing, and chatting away. Then they brought out a gorgeous cake—so beautiful and, oh, so delicious! People cheered, "Blow out the candle, come on, blow it out. Like this—blow!" My cousin just waved his hands, trying to grab the flame. I thought I'd help and blew it out for him. Instead of thanking me, everyone stared in disapproval and went, "Ohhhh!" Luckily, they got over it and served the cake.

I had never in my life tasted anything so delicious! After everyone got their slice, I noticed the rest of the cake was taken to the kitchen and put inside a large white box— the fridge. That night, when everyone was asleep, I tiptoed into the kitchen and helped myself to another big piece of that amazing cake.

Every summer, my sister Lex and I took turns staying with our aunt and uncle in the city. When it was my turn again, I was 14.

My aunt told my mom she wanted to make my *quinceañera* dress. They started planning the party. My mom sewed herself a dress the same color as mine: soft green. For my dad, she pieced together a shirt from two old ones—the sleeves made from the back panel of another. I was a bit embarrassed that they were spending money on a party we couldn't really afford, but my aunt had insisted on making the dress. The least my parents could do was provide a traditional meal from our home state.

They went to the city market for banana leaves to make Chiapaneco-style tamales. They also prepared *cochito enchilado* (spicy pork), though it came out a bit burnt—we didn't have an oven.

Weeks before the party, everyone was excited. Aunt and uncle, Mom and Dad—we all walked through the streets of Mexico City shopping for shoes. I trailed behind, silently keeping an eye on my little cousins. Nobody asked me, "Do you like these? What do you think?" Nope. I didn't get a vote. And I didn't like the shoes they chose—they were too pointy. I would've preferred something simpler, with a buckle. But I had no say, even though I was the birthday girl.

My dress, though made from nice fabric in a lovely color, didn't feel right. It had a proper bust seam, sure—but my aunt added some odd darts at the front that puffed out over the stomach (what for?). She also made a beaded capelet, beautifully embroidered by hand. "Look, my fingers are bleeding from all that beadwork!" she told me. "Oh, thank you, *tía*," I said.

So much work—and yet I didn't feel comfortable. I felt ungrateful.

My sister Clelia later said that on the day of the party, she saw me crying. "Why is she crying if it's her birthday?" she wondered.

I just felt awkward and ridiculous, with a quiet rebellion building inside me and no clue how to let it out. It was my fifteenth birthday, but I wasn't happy.

In the photo, I'm standing next to my mom, who looked beautiful in her matching dress. My dad is wearing his patched-up shirt. My aunt looked lovely in her maternity dress—she was expecting another baby.

Chapter 18 – From the Source

Here it is, my beloveds, so no one must tell you secondhand, and no one makes up things — this is the account of what happened to me. Who else would know it, if not me, the source? Some of the stories and anecdotes from my mother and father are directly from them. No fiction, no invention. Maybe a touch of exaggeration, like my dad saying, "I took out four." (I think it was only three guys he sent to the other side.) And that was in self-defense, since they wanted to kill him. But when he was yelling those things, it was because he'd already had a few *pulques* (a thick fermented drink from the agave plant). And we'd say, "*Shhh, Papá!* That's supposed to be a secret!"

And my mother might've exaggerated a bit when she said that, for her wedding preparations with my father, they'd sacrificed "*chorrocientas*" hens (roughly a zillion). She'd gesture with her hands toward a little tree near the washbasins and describe an imaginary procession of chickens hanging by the neck all the way there.

Maybe they exaggerated a little, but I don't. And as you read these memories, you'll see — if anything, I've left out details. Here it goes, before memory plays tricks on me.

At a recent family gathering, my niece Rebeca asked if it was true that I stayed living in Texcoco (the place where my children were born) because I had a debt to their father — that I was somehow bound to live with him because of that. *Of course not!* Where did they get that? I owed that man nothing!

The only reason we spent so long trapped in that life was *fear*. Pure fear. I lived in constant threat, terrified.

It was no way to live. What kind of future awaited my children? I was humiliated and judged by the neighbors, simply for being the woman of a man who, thanks to his money, could seduce as many as he wanted and set them up in their own homes.

My sisters and brother would visit sometimes, and they could see how unhappy I was. My youth had been stolen. I was 17 when he seduced me. My family kept reminding me I wasn't alone, that I could come back home. They'd help me raise my children — who were and are my whole life.

So, terrified but determined, I dared to return to my village, to the adobe house where I grew up. What joy to be back with my family! I didn't ask for much — just to live in peace, to see my children grow, to cook for my siblings, clean, wash, and do everything, but *with them*. Savoring the freedom, I settled in with my babies.

My sister Lex warned me that the man (I won't even say his name) would come for me. "*You stay firm,*" she said. "None of that going back to that life you're so ashamed of." "No way, I'd never go back," I told her. "Not even if he begs."

Oh, how naïve I was! Did I really think he'd just let me live in peace? Of course he showed up — to beg me to return. But he found me empowered and resolute. I wouldn't go back.

So, he used the most despicable tactic: he threatened to take my children if I didn't return. And I knew — with his money and power — he could do it. As he rambled on, flaunting his power, I stopped hearing his words. All I could do was hold Óscar and Luzi close. No one was taking them from me.

In tears, I returned to the life of captivity and shame.

Years passed. More children came (the younger ones now so grateful I went back, and the older ones too — we can't imagine life without any of them. They're all blessings, each one for the others — and especially for me).

But the escape plan remained alive. We had to be discreet. If I ran to my old home, he'd find us easily. So, we crafted a new plan.

Everything was carefully mapped out for a grand escape — that July morning of 1976. But even with all our precautions, something went wrong. Everything could have fallen apart. I could have lost my children. I could have died of grief.

Only one person could save us.

Wearing her invisible cape, my little wonder girl — my firstborn — came to our rescue.

Seven years earlier, she had saved us once before, literally bringing light into our darkest days. In Spanish, to give birth literally means *to give light*.

My mother, pregnant again, died during childbirth. The doctor had warned her not to have more children because she had a hernia the size of a baseball. But with each pregnancy, I was more alarmed by that hernia than her belly.

I was still a teenager, also pregnant — hidden, ashamed, unable to show my face. My *domingo siete* (pregnancy outside of marriage) was a stain on the family, on me. I couldn't walk around proudly with a belly like other moms. That's when my father came to my hideaway to break the awful news.

"Your mother is dead. She's at the hospital. They won't release her body."

I thought I'd die too. I begged God for it to be a bad dream, a mistake. I collapsed, drowning in guilt and grief. It was May 5. People said the hospital had neglected her because it was a holiday and only interns were working. They kept her body for six long days.

Those days were torture — emptiness, disbelief, endless tears. I drifted around the house like a ghost. My poor brother, my mom's favorite — what would become of him? I threw myself into chores, cleaning, washing, anything to exhaust myself to death.

May 10 — Mother's Day — was the bleakest we'd ever known.

Finally, on May 11, they released her body. Because of the state of decomposition, we couldn't even hold a proper wake. Just a brief prayer at the church. Then the burial.

It was a crude reality. My mother was gone. It wasn't a nightmare. There we were saying goodbye. I almost collapsed into the grave. My godmothers held me up, reminding me I had to stay strong — for my baby. Did I even remember I was pregnant? I felt like I no longer existed.

It surprised me that despite so much pain, so much work, so many prayers and sacrifices on hands and knees, somehow, I was still alive. I could still see my baby sisters playing, too young to understand. "How old are you?" they'd ask the youngest. "Cuatlo," she'd say, holding up four little fingers.

After the novena (a Catholic custom of nine days of mourning prayers), we took flowers and leftover candles to her grave — closing the ritual.

Then came May 21 — the Day of Our Lady of Light.

And it truly was a *day of light*.

The tears turned into joy. God sent us the miracle of life.

I gave birth — to María de la Luz. She arrived to light our shadows. She brought us back to life.

Beautiful, healthy, strong — she was born from my sorrow, but carried a purpose. She was here for a reason.

And she still had another mission.

Because as we prepared for the great escape years later, something went wrong.

Luzi had a friend at school whose father owned a moving truck. That was our means of escape. I begged him to keep our destination secret. He agreed. The plan was: he'd pick us up at 5:00 a.m. I didn't sleep that night. I packed the children's little bags, sold a few things, and told the neighbors we were going to Chiapas.

But 5:00 came. He didn't show.

5:10 — nothing.

5:15 — *nothing*.

Terror gripped me. What if, instead of the driver, my ex showed up?

We had one hope. My daughter.

Luzi knew where her friend's house was. She'd been there before. Could she find it alone in the dark? With trembling hands, I asked her to go.

She went.

The kids stood with their backpacks, and I stood praying like never before.

And then — on the quiet street — *we saw the truck.*

The driver... and my Luzi.

She did it. She saved us. *Again.*

She's my hero. My lighthouse in the dark.

We were born again, thanks to her courage.

Chapter 19 – Chapingo, Glorious Campus

Before it became the well-known Universidad Autónoma Chapingo, this marvelous center of learning was called the Escuela Nacional de Agricultura, or ENA. Our celebrated Álvaro Carrillo, composer of such beautiful songs as *Sabor a mí*, *Cancionero*, and *Andariego*, named his daughter Ena after the initials of his alma mater. Álvaro Carrillo—proudly a *chapinguero*.

That's where my father found steady work after fleeing Chiapas.

Our town, Boyeros, is found west of Chapingo.

To have the privilege of entering this amazing school, a student had to have a brilliant mind and be deeply resolute. To qualify for the scholarship, one had to come from limited means. All of that described my siblings—who had the joy of calling themselves *chapingueros*. But not me.

If I had passed the entrance exam for Chapingo, my life would have gone very differently. The story I'm telling you here would be something else entirely. For a long time, I felt dumb and inadequate for not passing that Machiavellian exam. But how could I have prepared? I didn't even have the tools to study!

At home, the only books we had were the Holy Bible and *One Thousand and One Nights*, which my dad would make me read before bed. At that time, we didn't have a radio—much less a TV.

There wasn't even a library in our town. I would have sworn the blasted exam was in a foreign language—like Chinese or Russian—because I didn't understand a single question. I didn't have a private place to read either. My mom would send me to the roof to study. She'd excuse me from doing the dishes so I could concentrate and go over the guide. That booklet might as well have been written in hieroglyphs—I didn't understand a single word. To avoid boredom, I would sing. Yes, sing commercials I'd heard from the neighbors' radios. My sisters would hear me singing, "Mamá, yo quiero galletas, que sean, que sean, Lili." One of them would complain, "Mami! Tell Margarita to come down and do the dishes! She's not studying, just singing and singing!"

There was another possibility—I could try to get a scholarship to go to teacher's college. That would've been wonderful. But where to look for such a scholarship?

My aunt Agustinita had a brother who worked at the Department of Education. My mom and I took several bus rides to Mexico City to look for him.

The city—so overwhelming! Total chaos! The office was hard to find. We finally got there but never had the pleasure of meeting the uncle. He was always too busy. The secretary would greet us with the usual, "Come back tomorrow; he can't see you today." We went back several times. Eventually, my mom gave up. The bus fares alone were cutting into our food money. We spent energy and money for nothing. There was no other choice—I had to find work. I was sixteen.

My first job was in a dry cleaner. The very first thing I did was burn a jacket. I'd never used an electric iron. At home we had an iron that used hot coals. We'd wait for the fire to burn down into glowing embers before heating the iron and preparing the clothes. I had no experience with steam irons or electric ones. I learned on the spot.

My next job seemed more glamorous —a clothing store with elegant displays and mannequins modeling the latest fashion. I felt like I'd leveled up. I had no idea what was about to happen to me. The store's owner—who also owned several other branches—couldn't take his eyes off me. He would end up being the father of my first four children. Yes, *that* man. The one I don't even want to name.

We lived in captivity in Texcoco for many years. I couldn't even visit my beloved siblings in Boyeros. Sometimes we'd sneak visits—like when I just *had* to go to my sister Feliza's quinceañera, even though it cost me a punishment afterward. That was before we finally made our Great Escape.

And escape we did! We started tasting freedom again. I hadn't actually gone to Chiapas, as I'd told the neighbors (to throw him off my trail). We took refuge at my sister Flor's house, in a new housing development near Chapingo. I hadn't mentioned Flor before because she arrived in our lives when she was already a young woman. She came looking for our dad—who was her dad too. We lived in such poverty, wearing such ragged clothes, that when she showed up with her pretty little skirt and go-go boots from the '70s, I was mesmerized. She was studying to be a bilingual secretary in Mexico City. So lucky! So beautiful! So stylish! My dad had told us we had more siblings in Chiapas, but we never imagined they'd come find us. It was thrilling!

On one visit, Flor came to stay. She had already earned her diploma as a bilingual secretary and brought with her a beautiful little boy—my nephew Jacob. She had also shown up with her "Sunday surprise."

Flor had no trouble finding work at Chapingo.

Luckily, the university had recently built a housing complex nearby, and she got a brand-new two-story house—a mansion, really, compared to the ones the local farmers had received. It had an indoor bathroom, laundry area, and even a shower!

That's where we landed after the Great Escape.

There, we met a young woman who also worked at Chapingo. Talking with her, I learned she wasn't happy with her job. All she did was manually enter grades, and her electric typewriter was just sitting there unused. She was losing her typing speed.

I thought, *Oh, if only I could practice on that machine.* It was like daydreaming.

One day, Mara (that was her name) said she'd been invited to a party but wasn't going to go because there'd be a pool, and she didn't have a swimsuit. So, I offered—despite never having made one before—to crochet her a bikini. I'd been crocheting scarves and things to sell, but a swimsuit? That was new.

She couldn't believe how good she looked in the mirror wearing that bikini. I could hardly believe it either!

She wanted to pay me. "Please, let me pay you, sis! I love it! You should make more to sell."

That's when I had an idea that would change my life: "Instead of paying me," I said, "how about letting me practice on your typewriter whenever you're not using it?"

"Of course!" she said. "It's all yours."

And *bam!* —that's how the doors to Chapingo opened for me. I started going every afternoon. I'd sneak out of the house with a scarf wrapped around my head, incognito, so nobody would recognize me.

Ay, de mi Llorona, Llorona, Llorona idolatrada... There I left my sorrows, Llorona, all along the promenade...

That's how I sang *La Llorona Chapinguera* as I walked to campus, tears of joy in my eyes. That pathway led to the main building, home to important offices like the rector's and the financial department. Next to it stood the famous Riverian Chapel, with murals on every wall—including the ceiling and windows—painted by the great Diego Rivera.

In front of the building is the Fountain of the Circassians. What a beautiful fountain, *Llorona*, called the Circassians, a place I remember from birthdays, *Llorona*, where students used to get dunked. (That's part of the lyrics to *La Llorona Chapinguera*—about the tradition of tossing students in the fountain on their birthdays.)

I didn't ask for more. Just being inside that building, typing on one of those machines, made me immensely happy.

The engineers and professors who passed by would greet me politely and warmly. One afternoon, Engineer Abel Aguilera—who my sister Lex knew well, since he'd been her professor—asked me kindly why I was always there, and whether I worked there. I told him shyly that I didn't—I was just practicing. He said he would talk to Professor Porras and see about getting me into the next round of hiring.

Never in my wildest dreams had I imagined I could work at Chapingo. I practically ran home, hoping Lex would visit soon so I could tell her the good news. I needed her support and advice.

Lex had been a secretary. She knew all the rules of spelling, typing, shorthand—and how to behave professionally. She took it upon herself to prepare me to compete with the top-secretarial graduates from the best academies.

She gave me dictations to take in shorthand—the squiggly symbols that looked like Arabic script—and drilled me on words people often misspell: *decision*, *discipline*, *indecisive*, and so on. She also taught me accent rules:

Esdrújulas (third-to-last syllable): always accented. *Próspero, última, cáscara.*

Agudas (last syllable): accented only if they end in N, S, or a vowel. *Canción, corazón, a través, terminó* (as opposed to *término*, which is esdrújula).

Graves/llanas (second-to-last syllable): accented if they do *not* end in N, S, or a vowel. *Lápiz* yes; *palabra* no.

There are more rules for diphthongs and triphthongs, but this isn't a grammar class. You can thank me later for the mini-lesson.

That's how my sister prepared me. And I had the honor, the joy, of entering the prestigious Universidad Autónoma Chapingo—not as a student, but as a lovely secretary.

At that time, a cumbia was trending:
What a lovely secretary the boss has... I wish I had one just like her...
My sisters said it was written just for me!

Oh, what love.

Thank you, Flor. Thank you, Lex. Thank you, Mara. Thank you, Engineer Aguilera.
But above all—thank you, God.

Chapter 20 – For my husband

Literal

A poem for Jack Gilson, by Mago Gilson (rhymed adaptation)

He came to me, a sacred sign,
A gift from Wise Men, a man so fine.
I begged them in my raw despair,
Love-sick, foolish, stripped and bare.

Alone, adrift, I wept and yearned,
For kisses lost and hugs unearned.
My lips held words they'd never share,
My ears cried out for love and care.

To give, receive—was it too much?
To feel romance, a tender touch?
I dreamt of stars and moonlit skies,
Of roses red, of lover's sighs.

Of every line from books I'd read,
Where love lives on, though pages shed.
My soul stood open, pure and wide,
With only hope to be my guide.

So, with my pen, I did compose,
In trembling lines, my longing rose.
"Dear Wise Men, grant this heart a flame,
A hand to hold, to share my name."

I placed that letter, sweet and true,
Inside my shoe, as dreamers do.
So kings might find it come the dawn—
And make my sorrow be withdrawn.

They heard me well that winter night,
January 6th, to my delight.

There stood my prince—no tale or lore,
But real and shining, I wanted no more.

Tall and gentle, eyes sky-blue,
A soul so kind, a mind so true.

He dazzled me beyond compare,
I lost my breath, my worldly care.

Like Aladdin, with magic grace,
He led me to another place.

"Come, take my hand," he said with light,
"I'll show you stars beyond your sight."

And that is how my heart was won,
My Adonis, my only one.

Note: I met Jack Gilson at the Chapingo Autonomous University on January 6th after having asked Los Santos Reyes. They had told me as a child that the Kings did not exist, but I continued to leave my note in my shoe.

The Kings always brought me little toys, but with that flesh and blood doll, I was happy forever and I did not ask for more.

Chapter 21 – My fascination

My fascination
by Mago Gilson

I arrived in Eugene
with dreams of my homeland,
with nostalgic eyes,
with mixed emotions,
a mind full of memories,
my English with an accent,
walking slowly.

And then I saw you,
I was singing a song
when I saw you.
I was feeling very sad
when I saw you,
and the peace I found in you
made me stay in Eugene.

People strolled
there, near you.
Children ran
happily toward you.

Your beauty was such
that I fell in love with you.
Now I want to live near you and,
in moments of solitude,
have you bring comfort to my soul.
I want to hear your silent murmur
and find peace in that sound.

Sitting on the banks of your flow,
dazed and simply watching
enchanted,
fascinated,

and maybe at twilight,
your sweet waters
will carry me home
to my beloved homeland.
But for now, I only want to stay here
to sing and to dream in Eugene,
close to you, my river,
forever my river,
my Willamette River.

Chapter 22 – The Three *Desgracias* (Sort Of)

God gave me the fortune, the responsibility, and the privilege of being the oldest of a bunch of sisters—and one brother. And although our mother left us far too soon, she gave me that great gift to help fill the void of her absence.

Many years have passed, and now we're able to accept that our mother died at such a young age. Somehow, we survived that indescribable pain. Only the love we share for one another has kept us going.

To speak of my sisters and brother would take a whole book for each of them. So, they'll each have to write their own story someday. I'll only share a few things, drawn from the heart and memory.

My little sister, who we lovingly call Lex—though our mother named her Lesvia—a source of jokes in school because of that name. So, we shortened it with affection, and Lex it has been ever since. She was born with the soul of a leader. Though I'm the eldest of the six, she's been our compass: calm, clear, thoughtful. Always mindful of "speaking proper Spanish," as she puts it. No more extra s's at the end of second-person verbs like *estuviste* instead of *estuvistes*, or *comiste* instead of *comistes*. She made sure we left behind those old habits, without ever mocking those who still speak with that older regional Spanish.

Because of our mother's absence, she began working at an early age—just like I did—but unlike me, she kept studying. She worked as a secretary by day, went to high school in the evenings, and took sewing classes too. And she never stopped looking after her little siblings.

I always say I owe her the lives of my children, because she has been like a second mother to them — nurse, counselor, confidant. I will always love, respect, and be grateful to my Lex.

When my mother was pregnant for the third time, the long-awaited baby boy arrived—my brother Fidel, our golden child. Growing up surrounded by sisters, he became a fiercely protective and perfectionist older brother. He was born with a natural gift for music, able to play various instruments entirely by ear. He can play the piano, organ, guitar, and marimba. And above all, his voice—what a gift!

He was also the pride of our mother, who beamed when her favorite son earned a scholarship for his secondary studies. From the day he was born, she knew he was exceptionally gifted. He breezed through his classes, barely needing to study, acing every exam almost with his eyes closed. He should've gone to work for NASA. He didn't have to study until dawn or as we say in Mexico *"quemarse las pestañas"*—to burn one's eyelashes—used for those who studied long nights by the light of a candle.

Every two years, like clockwork, our mom brought another sister into the world. After the joy of the baby boy, another little girl was born. It was always exciting when our dad took us to spend the night at our godmother's or a neighbor's house, because we knew that when we returned, a new bundle from the stork would be waiting.

I enjoyed this little Clelia —cinnamon-skinned, curly-haired, just like me. Lex and I took turns brushing her hair. I thought Lex didn't do it as nicely as I did, though she claimed I had no sense of style.

I made a dress for my sister Clelia that she loved so much, she refused to take it off—even to sleep or bathe. I had sewn it from an old cover that used to clothe our sewing machine. Yes, you heard that right—maybe we didn't have much, but that sewing machine had outfits! When my mom discarded the fabric, I saw its potential and asked if I could use it. "Of course," she said. "What are you going to make?" "A dress for the little one," I answered confidently.

Though the fabric was worn, it still had a charming floral pattern. I got to work, pleating what would become the skirt. When finished, it was so puffy it looked like it had a crinoline underneath. I double-lined the bodice for strength and stitched it together using our sewing machine, stretching my little legs to reach the pedal. When it was finally ready, my little sister lifted her arms eagerly, and I carefully stitched it closed along the back. No buttons, no zipper—just a snug little dress. Once she had it on, she danced around like a ballerina, showing her littler dress off.

Weeks passed, and she still wouldn't take it off. The dress became a second skin. By the time my mom forced her to remove it for a bath, it was practically fused to her. She had to use ointments, vapor rub, and warm water to loosen it—eventually peeling it away but taking some tender skin with it. To this day, my sister bears the little scar, like a tattoo, a memory of that beloved dress.

Two more years passed, and it was time again for us to pack up and go spend the night with our godmothers. Only this time, it wasn't necessary. Instead of the stork arriving at our house, they took my mother to a maternity hospital—which was hard for us to accept. The only thing that comforted us was knowing she'd come back with another little sister... or maybe this time, a little brother.

My poor father had to manage all by himself with that growing pile of children. Cooking for us turned out to be a true challenge. I remember watching him hustle around the kitchen, determined to make us some chilaquiles. Maybe he figured they'd be the easiest dish. He gave it his all, bless him—but they turned out so bland. He'd forgotten the salt! (Memory is funny like that —how it chooses certain moments to etch into your heart forever. For me, it's those unsalted chilaquiles.) Over the years, though, my father learned how to cook quite well.

Then the day came. My mother returned from the hospital with a soft bundle in her arms.

Our tíos from the town of Cooperativo came to visit us. They were curious to meet the new baby and hear how Mamá had done in the hospital. They got a good laugh watching Papá worry. He wasn't so sure the baby was ours. "How could they know which one was ours?" he asked, half-joking, half-suspicious. "There were hundreds of newborns in that place!"

But our tío just looked at the baby's face and said, "She's yours, alright. She's the spitting image of you."

That little girl born on November 20, 1960—right on the *Día de la Revolución Mexicana*—was our Feliza, who we lovingly call "Lichita."

And twenty-three years later, on that very same date, I gave birth to my own daughter. Her name is Amada—very loved.

Two more years passed, again. We had moved into our own house, with the smell of fresh earth, a beautiful picture window, twin trees in front, and plenty of land to grow vegetables. We had chickens, turkeys, ducks, pigs, and even a goat. On that land, we grew corn, beans, squash, potatoes, green beans, and other veggies.

Our mother decided to go to the hospital again—time for another sister! When she returned, we had a surprise for her: the ewe had given birth to a beautiful, woolly lamb. But the moment she stepped into the house, lamb or no lamb, our attention was all on the baby girl, who was and still is, very cute.

To name her, my dad had the grand idea of having me read from the Bible, and the first woman's name to appear would be hers. Of course, the first name that popped up wasn't the one he liked, but after a while—maybe after dozing off—he woke up just in time to hear "Sarah." And that's the name she got. For us, she became Sary.

Time passed, and it was time again. My mom was heading back to the hospital—no more home deliveries, the stork was now on sabbatical. But before I tell you about the birth of our youngest sister, I have to take a breath. Just remembering it gives me chills.

The night before February 11th, I can still see my mother furiously pedaling away at the sewing machine, trying to finish my PE uniform for school. She hadn't needed to make my regular school uniform—my Aunt Agustinita from the Cooperativo had made that one. It was perfect for my growing body, pink and beautiful, and I loved it. I polished my new shoes till they gleamed, and I was so in love with them I'd secretly kiss them when no one was looking. I wanted them to last forever.

The PE uniform required a blue skirt with three white ribbon stripes around the hem, a blouse, white shorts, and sneakers. My aunt offered to make this outfit too, but my mom insisted on doing it herself—not wanting to burden her sister-in-law. She sewed and sewed, but used so much fabric that it looked more like a folkloric dance skirt than a gym outfit. When I lifted the hem with both hands, it reached my head!

She finally finished and we both went to bed exhausted. But barely under the covers, she started to moan. I thought her legs hurt from so much sewing, but suddenly my dad got up and said he was going to fetch Doña Cleofas. My mom screamed, "NO! You help me!"

I was petrified. My eyes were as wide as saucers. I had no idea she was even pregnant—her belly always looked big!

And I still believed babies came from the stork, even though I was already in secondary school. I was very innocent. A few days earlier, my mom had tried to explain the *three desgracias*—the "three misfortunes" women face. I remember it like it was yesterday. We were making tortillas, the kitchen thick with smoke from the firewood. She probably chose that moment so the smoke could mask her awkwardness.

"It's time for you to know," she began solemnly, "that women go through three desgracias." I imagine that's how it was told to her too. "The first desgracia," she continued, "is that when a girl becomes a woman, she starts to bleed."

"What?! How?" I asked, incredulously.

"I can't say more—you'll find out soon enough," she replied seriously.

"And the second desgracia..." She hesitated. "That one happens when a woman gets married. On the wedding night, the man does something that... hurts a lot."

"What? What does he do?" I asked, now even more confused and scared.

"I can't tell you that either. You'll learn in time."

I was lost. I didn't understand a thing.

"And the third desgracia... is that babies are NOT brought by the stork!"

"What?! No way! I had just found out the Three Wise Men weren't real—now this? They don't come on a camel, a horse, and an elephant? And now the stork isn't real either?! Then who brings the babies?"

"We do. Women bring them into the world."

"But how?" I asked, stunned.

"They come out of us," she said, tossing another tortilla onto the hot griddle.

"Out of us?! But... through where?!"

She gave no hints. But there, in front of my astonished eyes, she gave birth. And in that moment, I realized—it wasn't a desgracia at all. That sweet little girl who was born on February 11th, the day of Our Lady of Lourdes (another name for the Virgin Mary), was a blessing.

From the Source

Chapter 23 – Like the Five Fingers of My Hand

Like the five fingers of my hand, that's how my five children are—each one beloved, held close to my heart. I close my fist, and there they are.

So alike, and yet so different. More than a mother could ever ask for from the fruit of her womb.

All I can do is thank the Creator, who gave me the means and the wisdom to guide them. To my sisters, too, I owe thanks—for their love, support, guidance, discipline, and example of perseverance.

Motherhood took me by surprise, right in the middle of my teenage years. Even so, my arms were ready to cradle my first child. My Luzi taught me how to be a mother. She brought me a happiness I didn't even know existed. On May 21, she was born—and I came back to life.

In the Mexican calendar, that day—May 21—is dedicated to *Nuestra Señora de la Luz*, Our Lady of Light. I had been thinking about names that could easily turn into affectionate nicknames: like Paty from Patricia, Leti from Leticia, Susi from Susana, Gaby from Gabriela. When I saw the name on the calendar, I didn't look any further. Her name had already been chosen: Luzi.

For me, there was never any of that planning—"I'll have this baby, raise them well, send them to the best schools," and all the things newlywed couples dream about when starting a family. No. My children came one by one, and I adapted each time, adjusting to the next and the next—maybe even neglecting the ones who came before. I've always felt I owed my firstborn a sister to play with, because after her came three boys, one after another, always off playing together in their own world of adventures and mischief. I'm forever grateful to my sister Lulú, who stepped into that role and became the first sister my Luzi had. Luzi may have received the first kisses and cuddles from her mother and aunties, but she was soon replaced—our affections shifted to the next baby.

On December 17, my Óscar was born. What a beautiful baby. Though he cried so much! And I couldn't give him the full attention I had given Luzi. I had diapers to wash and two babies to care for. Before diving into chores, I'd make sure he was nursed and had a clean diaper. But oh, how he cried! Maybe he had a colic. I never really knew. I didn't know how to burp babies. I never did that with any of them. To soothe him, his sweet little sister—still not even two years old—would rock his cradle and sing to him: "*No llode, no llode, no llode...*" asking him not to cry.

That boy grew up to be strong-willed, well-organized, and successful. When he served in the Navy in Japan, he became even more disciplined. He looked so handsome in uniform. But when he was sent to the Gulf War, my heart broke with fear. Those were days of anguish and endless tears.

At last, we could all breathe again when he returned, wiser and more experienced. I am a fortunate mother—to have a son who is a war veteran. But even more admirable than that, he is a wonderful father.

Then came my third child—another son. My sisters and I chose my children's names together. And by some strange coincidence, my children were always born on holidays—so there were no names listed on the calendar. Eddy was born on April 20, Good Friday. Had I gone by the calendar, he would've been named *Viernes* (Friday). Actually, that wouldn't have been so bad—like Robinson Crusoe's companion!

My sister Clelia had once dated a boy named Edgar. Also, my aunt Tere (my mom's only living sister, who lives in Chiapas) has two sons named Óscar and Edgar. So we went with that name, knowing we could call him Eddy, like the song Angélica María sings: *Eddy, Eddy.*

This boy might seem like the most serious of all, but then he'll surprise you—he's secretly hilarious. Oh, the stories we could tell about his mischief! Now they make us laugh, but when he almost burned down the house, it was no joke.

And what about the time he ruined everyone's chance to get ice cream? I had promised them that if they all got vaccinated without crying, I'd buy them cones. All was going well—until Eddy bolted. The nurses chased him through the clinic and finally found him hiding under a doctor's desk. They almost had to tie him down for the shot.

But aside from that, he grew up to be a fine young man—handsome and hardworking. Always neat and helpful around the house, always starting new projects. He reminds me of my father, always fixing things. And like his older brother, what I admire most about him is that he's an exceptional father.

A few years passed—because obviously, I didn't have enough children—and my fourth arrived, my third son, born on December 24. The calendar said *Nochebuena*, Christmas Eve. That wouldn't do for a name. On Clelia's suggestion—she always had boyfriends with nice names—we named our Christmas Eve baby *Víctor*. Oh, what a beautiful child! Truly—and it wasn't just a mother's love talking. Each of my children seemed more beautiful than the last. I could've rented them out for nativity scenes, but I didn't want them catching cold in just their diapers.

Víctor needed glasses, but I never realized it. He sat so close to the television because he couldn't see well. It wasn't until we came to this country that we were told he needed glasses. How embarrassing! But in our family, no one had ever needed them. My sister nicknamed him *Bambi* because of his big, beautiful eyes—and the movie was in style at the time. He grew into a kind, respectful, and empathetic young man. I could use so many adjectives to describe him, but like his brothers, what I admire most is that he's a wonderful dad.

And like the fingers on a hand—five of them—came the little pinky. The baby girl we had all been waiting for. Beautiful, adored, my *Amada*. She was born on November 20, the anniversary of the Mexican Revolution. The calendar said: *Día de la Rev. Mex.* Not exactly a pretty name for a little girl. *Amada* comes from the verb *amar*—to love. And it reminded me of the great Mexican poet Amado Nervo.

Just like her big sister Luzi brought joy to our lives, this youngest one became everyone's delight. She could've been the spoiled one—but I think I neglected her a bit. I often have these nagging thoughts that I could've done better. Give more attention. Been less strict and more loving. These regrets hurt me the most.

There's a cassette recording where we're all singing and laughing—my sister Lulú was there, playing the guitar. During the chaos, you hear a little voice: *"Mami, Víctor me torció mi dedo."* No one pays attention. She says it again: *"Mami, Víctor me torció mi dedo."* And then, more quietly, with a tired tone: *"Víctor me torció mi dedo."* You hear Víctor respond, *"Cállate escuincla chismosa."* My poor baby girl— no one gave her the attention she needed because Víctor twisted her finger and scolded her to keep quiet. And there are so many moments like that, clear evidence of my carelessness.

Another time, when our relatives from Mexico were visiting, we went to Washington Square Mall. Amid the crowds, suddenly, there she was—crying: *"I got lost and you didn't even notice!"* Oh, how painful. What a shame. My sweet little girl! And so many moments like these remind me of the ways I failed my *Amadita*.

And there's one that's especially sad, captured forever on video. They were all playing happily on the trampoline while I recorded. Since I was fascinated with the new camcorder, I was always recording. Suddenly, she bit her tongue. She came down, hand to her mouth, and said: *"Mami, me mordí la lengua."* And what did I say? *"Well, don't do that again. And tell your brothers to be more careful."*

But the worst part, I only just found out—is that I sold her stuffed animals in a garage sale. Among them, a plush toy her brother Óscar had sent her from Japan. *Can you forgive me, my darling?*

Only God, in His mercy, and His guardian angels protected us all and brought us to where we are today. I couldn't be prouder. My sweet *Amadita* is now a wonderful mother and an extraordinary human being.

Now that I've walked through these memories, I close my fist once more holding my five children close to my heart.

Chapter 24 – The Changes Life Brings

"*Como han pasado los años*," [Oh, how the years have passed] says a popular bolero, "the changes life brings."

And the changes in my life have been beautiful. My children are my pride, my joy, my blessing.

Just recently, my son Oscar called to ask if I'd be willing to give a talk for International Women's Day.

What an honor, that my son trusts me and believes in me enough to recommend me to speak to other women—and to men too—to inspire, encourage, and uplift.

Knowing everything we've been through: the struggles we've endured, the sacrifices, the humiliations—and the support we've received along the way—it's all been a lesson. We can humbly say that up to this point, God has brought us and blessed us.

Yes, it's been hard—everyone knows that—because if getting there, fighting, swimming against the current, and achieving these goals were easy, anyone could do it.

While most young people look forward, pursue their studies, and build a future, not everyone has those opportunities.

I didn't.

Working from a young age was my only choice.

Even though studying was always my dream.

The Autonomous University of Chapingo was right there, so close, within reach for the most capable.

That wasn't me.

My younger sisters and brother did get in. They passed Chapingo's difficult entrance exam and stayed afloat in that rigorous environment.

When students were weeded out year after year for low grades, my siblings kept their scholarships with excellent marks.

That university is truly a marvel.

I couldn't get in—not because I lacked the desire, but because I didn't pass the exam.

And that made me feel like the least intelligent of my sisters.

I never even made it to high school.

At sixteen, I had to leave home and find work.

And I got pregnant out of wedlock.

Still, even while raising my children, I carried a hunger and thirst for learning.

I devoured whatever books I could get my hands on.

I listened to educational programs—like the national radio hour on Sundays.

But there weren't many options.

I didn't know about adult education programs back then.

When we immigrated to this country, doors began to open—especially in education.

The access to schooling that I had been denied for lack of money in my homeland became possible here.

My children, despite the culture shock and language barrier, managed to learn English and keep pushing forward in school—all the way to college.

At the same time, I worked hard to get my GED. That was the first step toward higher education.

While I was studying, I cherished the opportunity to attend college.

It was wonderful!

I never wanted to stop.
I kept taking classes I liked.

I was so fascinated with learning, I couldn't believe I was part of that world.

Some classmates, seeing how many classes I was taking, told me to go talk to a counselor.

But I didn't understand why.

I thought counselors were for people with psychological problems!

So, I just kept studying.

Each new class gave me ideas.

I wanted to be a nutritionist, a PE teacher, an astronomy, and an oceanographer.

It was like being a little girl in a candy store—I wanted to try everything.

Eventually, I understood the real reason to see a counselor:

To help me figure out what to do with all these courses I was taking!

There were moments of frustration when I felt like giving up.

So, I went to see one of those counselors and told him I was too old (almost forty!) to be messing around with college.

And he said to me:

"You'll turn forty whether you like it or not. Wouldn't it be better to turn forty with a college degree under your belt?"

Wise words.

But doubts crept in again, like when one of my sons would come visit with my granddaughter and I'd think:

"I'm a grandma! What am I doing, acting like a schoolchild?"

I'd tell myself, "Go home and take care of your grandkids."

But then I'd remember what the counselor said. "The hard part is over. You can do this."

Getting that GED diploma was the most difficult step.

I'd been trying to earn it back in Mexico through an alternative high school degree preparation program. Those who felt ready went to Mexico City to take the exam.

I studied for months, then traveled into the city to take the test.

And I failed.

Again, and again.

I'd pass maybe two or three sections, but not the required five.

It crushed me every time.

I felt like I just wasn't smart enough.

When I got here and learned that you could get a GED in the U.S. too, I said to myself, "No time like the present. Let's go."

Even with the language barrier, even with the fear, I pushed through.

I think I had some trauma from failing that test in Mexico.

I even had dreams about it.

One time I dreamed the diploma was framed and hanging on the wall. In the dream I asked myself, "When did I pass those tests?"

Then I woke up.

No frame.

No GED.

"How hard could it be?" I thought.

"Just buckle down and study until you make it."

And you know what?

That GED was harder than earning my master's degree!

Taking classes with my kids was the best.

They saved their books for me, gave me advice, and recommended teachers.

When I finally understood what I needed to graduate, I took summer classes and extra credits to catch up.

Graduation day came.

It felt surreal—like a dream.

But it was real.

And I was graduating alongside my sons, Eddy and Oscar.

In the summer of 1998, I earned my master's degree in education.

There's a framed photo in my living room—with President Clinton and the three of us.

Yes, *that* President Clinton.

He was the guest speaker there to inspire the graduating class.

In his speech, he spoke about the importance of immigrants in this country.

He mentioned one immigrant in particular:

"A few years ago, she came here without even a high school diploma. Today she's receiving her master's degree. A round of applause, please. Her name is Mago Gilson."

Had he just said my name?

Was he really talking about me?

The cameras turned toward us.

Journalists surrounded us.

The news was on TV.

We were part of it.

It wasn't a dream.

There are photos from the newspapers, interviews, and framed memories on the wall of my home—reminders that the little girl who "wasn't smart enough" to pass the Chapingo entrance exam didn't lack intelligence.

She just lacked opportunities.

Family Album

(My mother before meeting my father) (My father more or less when he met my mother)

(My father and his sister) (The family recently arrived a CDMX from Chiapas)

(My mother and father)

(My sister Lex and I on baptism day)

(In Molino de las Flores with my grandmother Catalina (the one with the tape measure): Mamá, papá, Lex, Mago, and Fidel Rey)

(Oil stove)

(Our coal iron)

(The best part of my first communion were the sweet breads "panderuza")

(The family from Chiapas in Xochimilico)

(My father and mother with me on my *quinceañera*)

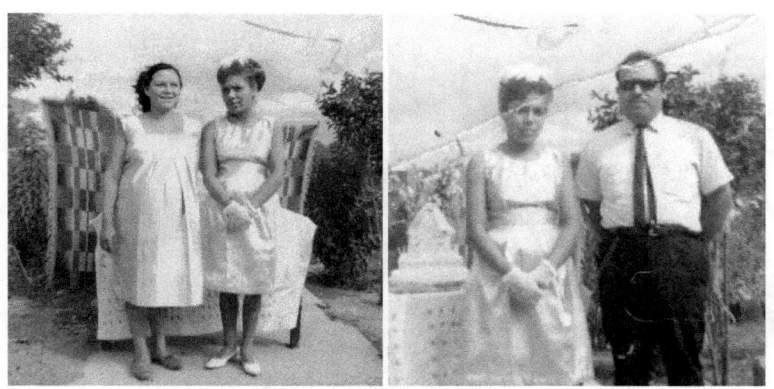

(My aunt Virginia y my uncle Chuy at my *quinceañera*)

(Any given Monday. Can you see the ravine in the background?)

(My sister Lex and I on a swing)

(Luzi and Óscar's baptism with aunt Lex the *madrina*.)

(Luzi, Óscar, and nephew Jacob, aunt Lex and me pregnant with Eddie)

(Eddy and Óscar in Texcoco)

(Peeling nopales in Boyeros with Víctor in the background)

(Eddy, Víctor and I on a playground at Luzi's school in Texcoco)

(Luzi wearing her pink colored uniform and aunt Lulu) (Luzi wearing her blue uniform for secondary school and I)

(Grandmother Adulfa, my mother's mother)

(Uncle Eloy and aunt Tere)

(Uncle Eloy y aunt Flor)

(Cousins: Eloycito, Ricardo, Blanca Flor and Luz Alba)

(A friend Chely and I, both pregnant, me with Amada)

(Chely and I, both breastfeeding our newborns)

(Víctor, Eddy, Óscar and Luzi at the house in Boyeros)

(Víctor at a primary school event)

(Eddy at a different school event)

(Eddy at a school event in Boyeros)

(Luzi graduating from primary school in Boyeros)

(Óscar doing homework at the house in Boyeros)

(Me showing off my dress in front of the house in Boyeros, *with a second floor*)

(The three musketeers: Lex, Clelia and Mago)

(My sister Feliza y I)

(Chapingo, Glorious Campus)

(Beautiful Mago in her twenties)

(Handsome Jack)

(Mago and Amada in Cornelius, Oregon)

(Víctor and Sara dancing the Bolonchón in Cornelius, Oregon)

(Sara, Lulú, Mago, Feliza, Lelis, y Lex at the Rose Garden, Portland, Oregon)

(My father building a water fountain at our house in Cornelius, Oregon)

(Óscar ready to set sail for the Navy, saying farewell)

(Eddy at a *quinceañera* in Cornelius, Oregon)

(Sisters)

(President Bill Clinton at my graduation in Portland State University)

(I got my masters in education!)

(I graduated with my sons Eddy and Óscar)

From the Source

Clinton praises immigrant's feat
A woman who came from Mexico in '80s receives a master's degree in education

By BILL GRAVES
of The Oregonian staff

Mago Gilson always hoped to become a role model after her 12-year climb to a college degree, but she never dreamed of being singled out in such a quick and lofty way.

President Clinton named the 46-year-old Mexican immigrant and two of her sons, Eddy and Oscar Gilson, during his speech Saturday at Portland State University, as examples of how hard immigrants work to gain higher education and the American Dream.

Becoming an American, Clinton said, means dreaming big dreams and passing them on to their children, like Mago Gilson did. He noted Gilson, of Cornelius, would pick up her master's in education in August, the president said. Then Clinton asked the three graduates to stand.

"I was very proud of my children," said Mago Gilson, still wearing her cap and gown three hours later. "They can see they can do it." Oscar Gilson said he will never forget the day he met the president.

> He was basing his speech on my mother. That makes him special to me. He cares for people like us.
>
> Oscar Gilson, whose family was included in President Clinton's speech

"He was basing his speech on my mother," he said. "That makes him special to me. He cares for people like us."

The three Gilsons, who met the president briefly before the ceremony, embarked on higher education together at Portland Community College more than six years ago. Mago Gilson had just earned her General Educational Development certificate, similar to a high school diploma. She was determined to keep going, with the help of scholarships, her husband and five children. Her parents, both deceased, had encouraged her to become a teacher. Her five sisters and one brother all had earned college degrees in Mexico.

Eddy Gilson managed a gasoline service station full time while going to school. He worked most weekends and never saw his wife and child. "I was always at school or work," he said.

Oscar Gilson entered college on the G.I. Bill after his discharge from the U.S. Navy. "I grew up feeling very dumb most of my life," he said.

But he soon realized he could succeed in school. Next month he will marry, and next fall he will begin his teaching career in Portland Public Schools.

Education is important, said Mago Gilson, who expects to teach high school Spanish in Portland next fall. She urged teen-agers to reach for good educations.

Then, she said, "maybe they will be lucky like us and get to meet the president."

(News clippings about the graduation)

Cornelius family cited at rites

By MIKE MLYNSKI
Of the Argus

CORNELIUS— Even after giving several interviews to television and print reporters during the past few days, Mago Gilson is still enthusiastic when describing the events of last weekend.

After all, she just graduated with a master's degree in education and was mentioned by President Clinton in his speech at the Portland State University graduation ceremony last week.

Gilson's sons, 27-year-old Oscar and 25-year-old Eddy, also graduated from PSU the same day and were mentioned in Clinton's remarks, which pointed out that immigrants can still achieve the American Dream.

With the family's permission, PSU officials offered the information on the Gilson family to the White House.

Clinton met personally with the family at a breakfast before the graduation.

"He (Clinton) knew our names, our degrees and all about us," Mago said. "He's awesome—he's so friendly."

"Yeah, I'm going golfing with him next week," Oscar chimed in after his mother's comments.

The honor of meeting the country's chief executive and being singled out by him in a speech hasn't meant that the Gilson's are taking themselves too seriously.

But the family's story is pretty awesome.

Margarita Moreno (Mago) was born in Southern Mexico and raised near Mexico City. She married Jack Gilson and came the United States in 1985.

Mago Gilson and sons, Oscar and Eddy, celebrate their PSU degrees.

The family moved to Cornelius in 1986. They bought a home and started to put down new roots.

Mago, 27-year-old Oscar, and 25-year-old Eddy started at Portland Community College together in 1992.

Oscar also received a master's degree in education while Eddy received a bachelor's degree in business administration.

"It was hard, but it's hard for everybody," Oscar said. "We didn't have the perfect language skills, self-esteem or money—but we had a goal."

"A lot of people like to make excuses," Eddy said. "I never liked the reading or homework in school, but without education it's hard to find a good job."

Mago Gilson said she likes learning so much that she might go after a doctorate.

"I'm strong—I don't feel old yet," Mago said.

You can bet that once she makes the decision, the PH.D. will follow for Mago Gilson.

(Víctor and I at my graduation ceremony)

(Eddy, Óscar and I at our graduation ceremony)

(Cousins in Tlaxcala, México)

(Eddy, Luzi, Amada, Víctor, and Óscar when Amada turned fifteen)

(The family in Hillsboro 2021)

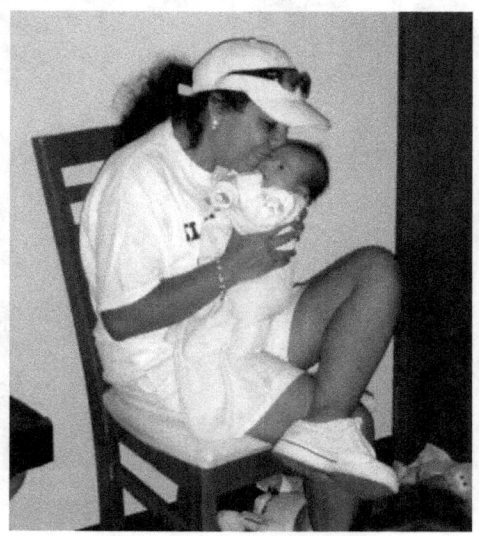

(GrandMago and Gabylucita)

(Mago and her "*cinco fantásticos*" 2021)

(Three generations)

(The apples of my eyes! Amada and Luzi)

(The last picture of aunt Quika, the one who convinced my father to flee from Chiapas, and I)

(The last picture of my uncle Eloy)

(We married in December 1980)

(Mago and Jack recently arrived in Oregon 1985)

www.ingramcontent.com/pod-product-compliance
Lightning Source LLC
LaVergne TN
LVHW051836080426
835512LV00018B/2911